G000152920

DERBYSHIRE
RAILWAYS

CLIVE HARDY

SUTTON PUBLISHING LIMITED

Sutton Publishing Limited
Phoenix Mill · Thrupp · Stroud
Gloucestershire · GL5 2BU

First published 1997

Reprinted 1998

Copyright © C.J. Hardy, 1997

Photograph, p. 1: A Stanier Black Five eases off
the Buxton Lime Co.'s plant at Peak Forest
(B. Blood); photograph, p. 3: Stanier 8F No.
48532 at Derby North Junction, 25 May 1966.
(C.M. & J.M. Bentley)

British Library Cataloguing in Publication Data
A catalogue record for this book is available from the
British Library.

ISBN 0-7509-1524-2

Typeset in 10/12 Perpetua.
Typesetting and origination by
Sutton Publishing Limited.
Printed in Great Britain by
Ebenezer Baylis, Worcester.

Ambergate in the snow. (M.L. Knighton Collection)

CONTENTS

INTRODUCTION

Derbyshire's early railways, better known as tramways or plateways, were often constructed to connect with a nearby canal thereby offering a reliable method of delivery to the nearest wharf for transfer. In 1778 the first tramway in the county was constructed. Using wooden rails it linked Shipley Colliery with the local canal. Ten years later Joseph Butler had a tramway built at Wingerworth to deliver materials to his furnaces. Butler's tramway was unique in that, for the first time in England, flanged rails were used above ground. Derbyshire men played key roles in the development of the country's transport systems. Benjamin Outram, born near Alfreton in 1764, was a skilled engineer who worked with William Jessop on the construction of the Cromford Canal in 1789, and who gained a reputation as a builder of tramways. In 1795 his 5 mile long tramway opened for traffic, linking Drury Low Colliery with the Little Eaton branch of the Derby Canal. By the turn of the century it was carrying around 40,000 tons of coal and stone a month. Other Outram lines included the Ticknall Tramway, which linked the quarries and limeworks at Calke Abbey with the Ashby Canal, and the 4 mile long Peak Forest Tramway built to link Doves Holes Dale, Holderness Quarry, Crist Quarry, several mills and lime kilns with the Peak Forest Canal at Bugsworth. Outram settled for a gauge of 4 ft 2 in, possibly because he was influenced by the farm and mining vehicles then in use in the area. The rails were 'L' section throughout, except for road crossings where 'U' sections were used, and were cast in 3 ft sections.

On 29 May 1830 the first section of the Cromford & High Peak Railway opened between Cromford Wharf and Hurdlow; the Hurdlow to Whaley Bridge section opened on 6 July 1831. Built over difficult terrain, the line required nine rope-worked inclines where wagons had to be raised and lowered using stationary winding engines. But the C&HPR offered a through route between the East Midlands and South Lancashire as well as an outlet for local coals and stone; in the early years it owned the infrastructure but allowed local and public hauliers to transport goods using their own horses and wagons – a sort of 1830s equivalent to Railtrack. The main problem confronting the railway was that from 1833 the inclines were restricted to handling just two wagons at a time in each direction. This caused chaos; traffic backed up the entire length of the line, wagons taking up to two days to travel the 30-odd miles from one end to the other. The C&HPR remained in splendid isolation from the rest of the growing rail network until 1853 when a 1 mile long spur opened from Cromford Wharf to a junction with the Manchester, Buxton, Matlock & Midlands Junction Railway. The northern end of the line gained a rail outlet in 1857 with the opening of the Stockport, Disley & Whaley Bridge Railway. But the C&HPR was always short of cash. In 1842 the company had debts of £47,000 and even with rail outlets at both ends there was never enough money to carry out all the necessary improvements. In 1862 the line was leased to, and in 1887 amalgamated with, the LNWR, who made several improvements over the years including track realignments and route deviations. But the C&HPR was never a conventional railway, retaining to the very end a unique character bordering on the eccentric.

The history of main line railways in the county begins during the 1830s. The Erewash coalmasters had enjoyed a near monopoly of the East Midlands coal trade but the opening of the Leicester & Swanningham Railway in July 1832 had enabled Bagworth, Ibstock and Whitwick Collieries to undercut Erewash prices by up to 10s a ton in Leicester. A few weeks later, the coalmasters resolved 'to attempt to lay a railway from these collieries to the town of Leicester'. The Midland Counties Railway was born. By the time the Parliamentary notices were deposited in November 1833, the MCR proposals were for a line connecting Pinxton and Leicester with additional lines from Trent to both Derby and Nottingham. Also included was a proposal for a link with the London & Birmingham Railway at Rugby. Further changes came in 1835 with a proposal to extend the line from Pinxton to join up with the North Midland Railway at either Clay Cross or Chesterfield. The NMR had issued its prospectus in September 1835 for the construction of a £1,250,000 line 72 miles long connecting Derby and Leeds. The NMR Act received Royal Assent on 4 July 1836, the MCR having been authorized on 21 June. The NMR was also authorized to construct a line between Sheffield and Rotherham but by now its main strategy was to connect with the Birmingham & Derby Junction Railway and possibly the L&BR. This would enable the NMR to offer a Leeds–London service without using the MCR. The NMR perceived the northern extension of the MCR as a direct threat to the southern section of its line to Derby. With its powerful and influential backers, the NMR was in no mood to take prisoners and succeeded in forcing the MCR to abandon the whole of its Erewash Valley line in exchange for Parliamentary approval for what remained. The MCR tried again to build the Erewash Valley line, issuing a prospectus in 1843, and although permission was obtained, nothing was done until 1847 by which time the MCR had merged into the Midland Railway.

The Birmingham & Derby Junction Railway, also projected in 1835, proposed an end-on connection with the NMR at Derby, the route to Birmingham being via Burton-on-Trent and Tamworth to Stechford where trains would then run over the L&BR to Curzon Street station. There would be connections with the Birmingham & Gloucester Railway and a branch from Whitacre to the L&BR at Hampton-in-Arden. This branch was a direct challenge to the MCR's intended connection with the L&BR at Rugby. Naturally the MCR raised objections. The B&DJR responded by offering to axe the Whitacre–Hampton branch in return for the MCR axing its Pinxton–Clay Cross line. The MCR accepted. However, when the B&DJR solicitors submitted for approval the proposals for the main line, they also submitted the Whitacre–Hampton branch as a separate company. Both Bills received the Royal Assent on 19 May 1836, whereupon that same day the companies united under an Act of Incorporation. The B&DJR had achieved its aims and once again the MCR had been on the receiving end.

The position at Derby was that the NMR and the B&DJR would be using a joint station. It wasn't the only thing they shared; George and Robert Stephenson were joint engineers to both companies. George Stephenson had also been active in the promotion of both companies and had amassed business interests along the route of the NMR with coal mines at Clay Cross and lime quarries around Ambergate. However, the MCR remained isolated with a separate terminus. It was Richard Wright, the Mayor of Derby, who suggested that the MCR should join the NMR and the B&DJR in sharing a station. A site was offered on The Holmes near the River Derwent and in June 1838 agreement was reached, Francis Thompson being appointed architect for the tri-junct station.

By the mid-1840s the MCR and the B&DJR were in direct competition for traffic between Derby and London. Despite having the shorter route, the MCR continued to lose out to the B&DJR as the latter enjoyed a cosy relationship with the NMR. A price war broke out: both companies cut fares and the B&DJR finished up in court over its pricing policy. The fighting had to stop as all three companies were suffering, and George Hudson of the NMR proposed their amalgamation. The Great Midland Amalgamation Bill received Royal Assent on 10 May 1844 and the Midland Railway Company came into being, Derby being the natural location for its administrative headquarters and workshops. Matthew Kirtley, formerly of the B&DJR, was appointed Locomotive and Carriage & Wagon Superintendent at a salary of £250. For thirty years the Midland Railway dominated the south of the county. The North Staffordshire Railway's line between Uttoxeter and Burton-upon-Trent opened for traffic on 11 September 1848, and in July 1849 an agreement was reached enabling the NSR to use Derby station via a junction at Willington for an annual rent of £2,000.

In March 1872 the LNWR began running passenger services into Derby, goods trains having started on 1 January. The LNWR had its own goods facilities and agents as well as a three road loco shed. Its routes in the county would eventually include Buxton–Manchester via Whaley Bridge, and from 1899 a line to the NSR at Ashbourne by way of a junction at Parsley Hay on the C&HPR. In September 1847 the Erewash Valley line was commissioned. This line later became a main route to the north. Its numerous colliery branches resulted in a massive amount of coal traffic, the development of Toton sidings, and the eventual need for quadruple tracks.

As well as dominating the south of the county, the Midland was desperate to gain a foothold in Manchester. The MBM&MJR opened its first stretch of line between Ambergate and Rowsley in June 1849, with a plan to join up with the Manchester & Birmingham Railway at Stockport. Unfortunately the M&BR was taken over by the LNWR, who had no intention of letting the Midland anywhere near Manchester. Another problem for the Midland was that, with itself, the LNWR was joint leaseholder of the MBM&MJR and also a shareholder although an agreement had been reached for the Midland to work the line for a period of nineteen years. In 1863 the Midland opened its line from Rowsley to Buxton. However, the problem of getting into Manchester remained, the preferred routes being under LNWR or Manchester, Sheffield & Lincoln control. A chance meeting between officers of the Midland and the MS&L resolved the matter. Strapped for cash, the MS&L agreed that in exchange for trackage rights over parts of the Midland system, the Midland could have access into Manchester from New Mills, the link being completed in 1867.

There was one problem yet to be faced. The LNWR still had an interest in the Ambergate–Rowsley section, and with the lease due to expire in 1871 there was a possibility of Euston gaining control thus leaving the Rowsley–New Mills line isolated from the rest of the Midland. Plans were drawn up so that if push came to shove a line could be constructed from Rowsley to connect with the Duffield–Wirksworth branch. However, the LNWR decided to withdraw from the MBM&MJR, and the line became part of the Midland in 1871.

In 1865, in the south of the county, the Trent–Weston-on-Trent line was authorized. It opened in 1869 and was extended to join the main line from Derby to Birmingham at Stenson Junction in 1873.

In 1878 the Midland was at last faced with a rival on its own doorstep when the Great Northern Railway commenced services from a connection with the NSR at Egginton Junction, then by way of Etwall, Mickleover, Derby Friargate, Breadsall, West Hallam, and Ilkeston to Nottingham London Road. Rivalry between the GNR and the Midland went back to the 1840s when George Hudson delayed the passage of the GNR Bill through Parliament. In the early 1850s the GNR was again on the receiving end of Midland hostility when a legal loophole was found to prevent it exercising certain running powers over the Midland from Colwick Junction to Nottingham. Authorized in 1872, the GNR line through Derby was just one phase in an expansion programme designed to net the company a share of the lucrative coal traffic from the Nottinghamshire and Derbyshire coalfield. It was also payback to the Midland for its cancellation of GNR running powers following the opening of St Pancras. In return for running powers over certain routes, the GNR had allowed the Midland to use Kings Cross while St Pancras was under construction. Other GNR lines to be built were between Colwick and Pinxton (including a sorting sidings at Eastwood) and along the Leen Valley.

The outbreak of the First World War had an immediate effect on the railways. Within forty-eight hours of the declaration of war the Midland had cancelled all excursion trains as the railways were placed under government regulation and control. Within two weeks normal passenger and goods services were taking second place to the needs of the military. On 15 August alone the Midland ran sixty-five specials from the Derby and Burton-on-Trent area on behalf of the War Department. As the war progressed a number of branch line stations lost their passenger facilities in the interests of war economy, while on the main lines services were cut to around half the prewar mileage. The war brought with it one of the greatest social upheavals in the country's recent history; because of severe manpower shortages women were allowed to take jobs previously considered a male reserve. There were lady tram drivers and conductresses, chauffeurs and machine operators. On the railways women were employed as engine cleaners and coal stackers, but they also worked in railway workshops given over to munitions production. Derby's contribution included modifying 6,000 railway vehicles for service overseas, manufacturing eight ambulance trains, stamping components for rifles and producing parts for howitzers and field guns. The women on munitions work renovated brass cartridge cases for 18-pdr field guns, working in a special shop segregated from male employees.

After the war the economies achieved by operating a unified railway network were not lost on the government of the day. Instead of going for nationalization, however, the 1921 Act resulted on 1 January 1923 in the creation of the Big Four. In Derbyshire this effectively meant that the lines formerly belonging to the NSR, the LNWR and the Midland joined together as part of the London Midland & Scottish Railway, while those of the GNR and the GCR formed part of the London & North Eastern Railway.

By the late 1920s the railways were suffering serious competition from bus and lorry operators, many of these companies having started up after the war using ex-War Department vehicles bought at knock-down prices. The motor industry was quick to meet the demand for new vehicles. In 1921 Dennis introduced its thirty-seat charabanc powered by a 40 bhp engine. Also from that year the Bristol Tramway & Carriage Company began supplying other bus companies with chassis. In 1928 BTCC was asked to supply 130 chassis to United Automobile Services, the country's largest independent operator. In 1931 Bedford Motors built its first vehicle, a WHB model with a fourteen-seat body work from the Waveney Company. This was followed by a twenty-seater in both bus and coach forms. Sales of Bedford buses rocketed, from 161 in 1931 to 630 in 1938. The Big Four bought shares in or took over bus companies in an attempt to keep the competition in-house. Inevitably, some branch line passenger services fell by the wayside. Among Derbyshire stations to lose their services were Melbourne, Chellaston & Swarkestone, Coxbench, Little Eaton, Denby and Ripley.

On 3 September 1939 two decades of peace were shattered by the German invasion of Poland. Once again the railways were placed under government control, this time under the auspices of the Railway Executive. One of the outcomes of the German Navy's devastating U-boat campaign was the introduction of fuel rationing. The railways became the only effective means of moving goods in bulk and people in quantity around the country. However, ordinary scheduled passenger services suffered; they became slow and unpunctual as speed restrictions were imposed to conserve fuel, and they were liable to cancellation with little or no notice.

By the end of the war the railway network was in a run-down state, as maintenance had been kept to a minimum; locomotives, rolling stock and infrastructure were for the most part worn out. In 1945 the incoming Labour Government announced its intention to nationalize transport, though the LMS fought against it. In the months leading up to nationalization more branch line passenger service withdrawals took place, some of them due no doubt to the continuing shortage of coal. On 16 June 1947 the LMS announced the temporary closing of stations to passengers on the Wirksworth branch, permanent closure following on 1 January 1949. Other LMS stations to lose passenger services included Butterley, Pinxton & Selston and Ilkeston Town. On the formation of British Railways, all LMS lines in the county became part of the London Midland Region, while those formerly belonging to the LNER were allocated to the Eastern Region. There was some tinkering with this, for on 2 April 1950 all ER lines west of Nottingham were transferred to the LMR. More passenger stations were closed in the early 1950s including, in 1951 Higher Buxton and the former GCR stations at Bolsover South, Scarcliffe and Chesterfield Market Place. In 1954 it was the turn of Killamarsh Central and all the stations on the former LNWR Ashbourne branch and the connecting NS line to Uttoxeter.

The early years of BR saw Derby Works as busy as ever. In 1951 No. 73000, the first of 125 standard Class 5 mixed traffic 4–6–0s was completed. As well as continuing to build steam locomotives, the works followed its involvement in the construction of the LMS's pioneering main line diesel-electrics with the Fell diesel-mechanical locomotive No. 10100. After catching fire at Manchester Central, this locomotive was withdrawn on 21 June 1958, by which time BR had already taken the decision to push through a programme of dieselization and to withdraw all steam locomotives by 1980 at the latest.

In 1958 Derby found itself engaged in the task of producing two types of diesels concurrently, the Type 2 1,160 bhp Bo-Bo and the Peak Class 2,300 bhp Type 4s. The C&W was constructing BR Mk 1 coaching stock introduced in 1951, of which over 1,000 were completed by the end of 1955. In April 1954 the C&W turned out its first lightweight railcars in two-car sets, followed in October 1956 by the first three-car set. By the end of October 1959 the works had completed 1,000 railcars, of which around 500 had been built during the previous twenty-one months. The 1960s ushered in yet more attempts at modernization including colour lights, the introduction of power boxes, and the proposed electrification of main lines with associated improvements to trackwork to allow greater line speeds. But it was already the age of the motor car, the pro-road transport government of the day having embarked on a programme of motorways, dual carriageways and bypasses.

The British Railways Board was formed under the Transport Act 1962, replacing the British Transport Commission which had managed the railways since nationalization. The chairman was Dr Richard Beeching. Beeching's infamous report, readily accepted by the government, was the kiss of death for much of BR.

Closures were announced with indecent haste, possibly in an attempt to stifle local opposition. Nottingham Victoria–Derby Friargate services ended on 5 September 1964, and on the former Midland main line from Derby to Manchester all stations north of Matlock up to Chinley went on 6 March 1967.

Steam traction finally disappeared from BR in 1968. Derby Works had carried out its last official repair to a steam engine in 1963, but was still busy in 1968 refurbishing and repairing diesels, though new construction had ended in April 1967 with the completion of No. D7677. The C&W Works was at capacity building Mk 2 passenger vehicles introduced in 1964. The Mk 2 was produced in seven variants, the works building no fewer than 1,892 units. In 1975 production switched to the Mk 3, which had been designed to run at 125 mph and from 1976 was incorporated into HST Class 253 sets, followed in 1977 by Class 254.

In 1963 locomotive and carriage and wagon works were separated from the rest of the business to become British Railways Workshops. Derby was chosen as the headquarters of the new organisation, and remained so after 1968 when workshops were renamed British Rail Engineering Ltd. In 1985 Derby was designated the main bogie manufacturing centre for BREL. Under the Conservative Government's privatization programme BREL was quickly disposed of, sold in 1989 to a consortium of British and Swedish engineering firms. In 1992 the Swedish firm ABB bought out its partners and assumed full control. The workforce has dropped from 7,500 in 1977 to around 2,000 today. The engineering group to which the works now belongs is involved in competitive tendering to supply new generation trains for both domestic and export customers, rolling stock for underground railways and supertrams for the new light railway lines.

The rail map of Derbyshire has changed dramatically over the last thirty years or so. From Derby the lines west to Nottingham and thence to London, south-west to Birmingham and north to Sheffield are open and might one day be electrified. Along the eastern edge of the county the Erewash Valley line remains in use though the only passenger station on it is Alfreton & Mansfield Parkway. The other main line remaining intact is the heavily used former Midland line between Sheffield and Manchester via Chinley. Several other lines are at present freight only, serving collieries, quarries and power stations. Of these, those in the Buxton area are witnessing a revival in traffic. It was announced in April 1997 that the Tilcon plant at Bredbury will be reopening to rail traffic from Tunstead and extra trains are expected to run in connection with road projects in Cheshire and the second runway at Manchester Airport. Since privatization English Welsh & Scottish Railways has committed itself to winning freight back from the roads. On 26 September 1996 the first train of steel pipes in twenty years ran from Stanton. The switch to rail came after a visit by EWS supremo Ed Burkhardt, the deal negotiated in ten days. EWS has every chance of winning back traffic as it is free to negotiate with potential customers; its predecessors were often hampered by Treasury and government requirements and archaic working practices, which together made rail an unattractive option to many businesses. EWS is the first operator to be awarded a four-fold increase in its track grant to 20p per mile. The grant is paid by the government to freight forwarders transferring from road to rail, to be set against Railtrack's track access charges. Grants are also to be made towards the capital costs of rolling stock and other equipment in cases where the traffic would otherwise go by road.

I hope that this introduction has helped to set the scene for what follows in the book. So sit back, turn the pages and enjoy this brief look into the history, and perhaps the future, of Derbyshire's railways.

AROUND DERBY

Derby tri-junct station as drawn by J.F. Burrell, c. 1842. The station was designed by Francis Thompson and built at a contract price of £39,986 by Thomas Jackson of Pimlico, London. Burrell's drawing shows the main entrance with its Venetian window and one of the subsidiary entrances (where the cows are).
(Author's Collection)

Detailed interior drawing of Derby station by Samuel Russell, 1841. Russell was commissioned by the architect to record the stations of the NMR. The train at the north end of the platform belongs to the MCR, although an NMR train can be seen in the background. Shunting was done using manpower, individual coaches and wagons being switched from one track to another by means of turntables. The station was lit by no fewer than 216 gas lamps. The MCR was the first to run trains out of the station when its line to Nottingham was officially opened on 30 May 1839. The B&DJR followed a few months later when its line from Derby to Hampton opened to traffic on 12 August. Last but by no means least came the NMR. Though George Stephenson had gone for easy gradients, the line to Leeds had involved the construction of seven tunnels, two hundred bridges including river crossings, deep cuttings and the building of twenty-six stations, and costs escalated to around £3,000,000. The first NMR train out of Derby left at 0915 hrs on 11 May 1840, consisting of four first- and two second-class carriages hauled by two locomotives, the pilot engine being driven by Robert Stephenson. The line was open as far as Masborough, and Stephenson brought the train in on time. The same could not be said for the first train from Masborough to Derby. It arrived 1 hour 45 minutes late. Among the dignitaries on board were George Stephenson and George Hudson. (Author's Collection)

Five Arches railway bridge to the immediate north of the station still carries the tracks over the River Derwent. When this drawing was made Derby was an open station, which just goes to prove that Railtrack's open station policy is nothing new. However, trains arriving from the north were detained at a specially built platform on the bridge so that tickets could be inspected. It is rumoured that more than one person made the mistake of alighting here only to finish up in the river. A similar inspection platform existed at the other end of the station for trains arriving from the west. Five Arches was later widened to take more tracks. (Author's Collection)

The frontage of Derby station in the early 1890s. The two-storey block on the right-hand side was completed in 1857 to a design by company architect John Sanders. It housed the shareholders' room on the upper floor, the ground floor being occupied by the Members Institute complete with classrooms, library and reading room. (Author's Collection)

Cavalry are deployed in Station Square, Derby, during the rail strike, 20 August 1911. The strike was typical of a number that occurred in 1911 and 1912 when Syndicalism was all the rage in the trades union movement. Syndicalism had its origins in the Anarchist movement in France and required a pluralist type of industrial organization, in which a federation of trades unions would replace the bourgeois parliamentary system. They believed they could fight their class struggle by means of general strikes thus bringing the government to its knees. They were wrong. In this picture the main station building is straight ahead, Nelson Street is to the left and the covered footbridge leads to the Locomotive Works. (NRM/DY9642)

'Who's next for promotion?' The busy telegraph office at Derby in the days when messages to and from headquarters were transmitted by morse code. (M.L. Knighton Collection)

Inside the trainshed. Both pictures are official photographs, the top dating from June 1911, the bottom from March 1920. They were taken on platform 2 looking south; the main entrance, dining and refreshment rooms situated on platform 1 are to the right. Note also the unusual signal arms owing to restricted clearance. The trainshed was damaged by enemy bombs during the Second World War, the remains being demolished in 1952 under a £200,000 modernization programme. (Top picture NRM/DY 9507. Bottom picture M.L. Knighton Collection)

His Grace the Duke of Devonshire inspecting troops on the station forecourt on a murky day in November 1940. (*Derby Evening Telegraph*)

The scene of destruction at Derby Midland following the air raid of 15 January 1941. HE bombs destroyed a 300 ft section of the trainshed roof and gouged out a 70 ft length of platform 6. A footbridge and the luggage subway were also badly damaged. Given the extent of the destruction, casualties were light: four passengers and two railwaymen killed and eight people injured. (LMS Official, M.L. Knighton Collection)

Both these photographs were taken just a few days after the air raid, and show the repairs to platform 6. New stairways have been constructed and the platform rebuilt using heavy timbers. Note the damage to the trainshed roof and to windows in the roof of old No. 2 engine shed. (Author's Collection)

The LMS fuel economy exhibition coach was doing the rounds in 1943 and was at Derby on 20 August. Visitors were given tips on how to reduce household consumption of coal, gas and hot water in aid of the war effort. 'Remember! The less hot water you use the more hot water for Adolf!' (Author's Collection)

A special troop train carrying former Far East prisoners of war pauses in Derby so the lads can get a wad and a brew, 18 October 1945. Note the poster advertising factories and factory sites at Trafford Park. (*Derby Evening Telegraph*)

Blowing off nicely, Jubilee Class 4–6–0 No. 45588 *Kashmir* heads a west-bound freight past London Road Junction at 0752 hrs on 19 April 1963. (Cliff Hudson)

The gantry at the north end of the station, June 1903. At this time the fronts of both stop and distance signals were painted red, the only difference between them being the cut out end. On the reverse side home signals had black roundels while distants had a black horizontal stripe. Some signals carried route indications, such as those for platforms 3, 4 and 6. Others had letters painted on them: P for passenger lines, G for goods lines. It was the LNWR back in the 1860s who pioneered a system for identifying semaphores by attaching rings to the arms of signals controlling slow or goods lines so that they could be readily distinguished from main line signals. In 1906 the Midland changed the paint scheme on the back of home signals to a black vertical stripe, adopting a similar style for distants in 1911. (M.L. Knighton Collection)

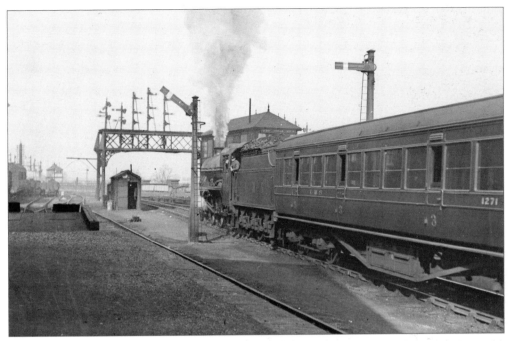

Heading north, Jubilee No. 5585 *Hyderabad* pulls confidently out of platform 2 and heads for Five Arches bridge, 13 March 1938. Derby station north signalbox is immediately behind the engine. Derby Junction box is in the background. (C.M. & J.M. Bentley)

Hoovers No. 50010 *Monarch* and No. 50048 *Dauntless* head off in the direction of Derby shed after working an RPPR railtour from Paddington on 18 March 1978. Arriving at 1221 hrs the Class 50s were detached and replaced by a pair of Class 20s for the next leg of the trip – a return working to Matlock. Both 50s have an interesting record. *Dauntless* was almost withdrawn before she was accepted into traffic by BR as she constantly failed through loss of power. *Monarch*'s claim to fame is that her fuel supply system had to be stripped out and replaced before she too was accepted. Neither survived into preservation. (Tony Griffin)

No. 1 shed, the former North Midland roundhouse, designed by the enigmatic Francis Thompson and built in 1839. The building is polygonal in shape with sixteen stalls situated round a central turntable. The roundhouse sports a superb lantern-topped pointed roof, which is supported on cast-iron columns and rises some 48 ft 10 in above rail height. When built there was sufficient accommodation for about thirty engines. By the time this picture was taken in 1905 the shed had been relegated to a repair facility. It was in regular use into the 1980s for the repair of breakdown cranes, making it the oldest roundhouse in the world still in regular use. (NRM/DY2743)

A view of the north end of Derby station taken from the works footbridge, *c.* 1890. The coaling stage is on the left while on the extreme right is the former MCR engine shed enjoying a new lease of life as a stores building. The centre road leads into No. 1 shed. (MR Official, Author's Collection)

No. 4 shed opened in early 1890 having cost £29,800 to build, and featured two 50 ft Cowan Sheldon turntables. There were plans to build a second twin turntable shed but the idea was shelved in favour of a single 60 ft turntable with radiating tracks out in the open. The picture must have been taken shortly after the shed opened. (MR Official, Author's Collection)

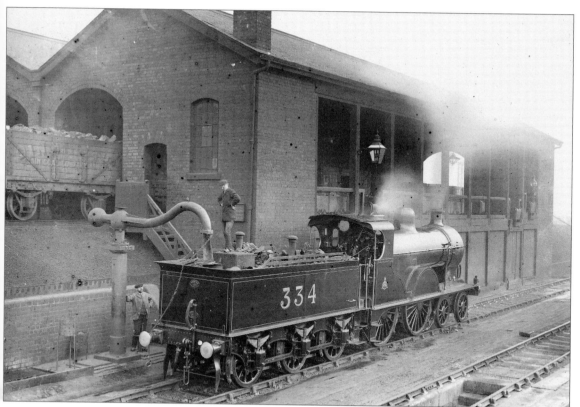

The Midland's photographer was having a busy day at the coaling stage near No. 4 shed, 25 November 1909. Having already photographed Deeley 990 Class 4–4–0 No. 993 taking water, he then turned his camera on H boilered 4–4–0 No. 334, which would soon be followed on to the plant by 4–4–0 No. 338. (NRM/DY2114)

Jubilee Class 4–6–0 No. 5618 *New Hebrides* and 2P 4–4–0 No. 418, stabled around the 60 ft Eastwood Swingler & Co. turntable, bathe in the glow of early afternoon sunlight, 13 March 1938. (C.M. & J.M. Bentley)

Kirtley and early Johnson locomotives arrayed outside No. 2 shed in the 1880s, including 0–6–0 goods engines, 2–4–0s, tank engines and what might be the Derby breakdown train. (Author's Collection)

Matthew Kirtley at his home at Litchurch Grange with his wife, Ann, and daughters, Emily and Elizabeth, late 1860s. Under his guidance Derby shops were transformed. As well as continuing with repair and maintenance work, an expansion programme soon gave Derby the capacity to construct new locomotives and rolling stock. In 1851 No. 147, an inside-framed 0–6–0 goods tender engine, emerged from Derby Works, the first of 2,941 new steam locomotives to be built there. By 1862 the workshops employed over 2,000 people; without doubt the coming of the railway had been the catalyst that accelerated Derby's growth from an insignificant county town to a major industrial centre. (Author's Collection)

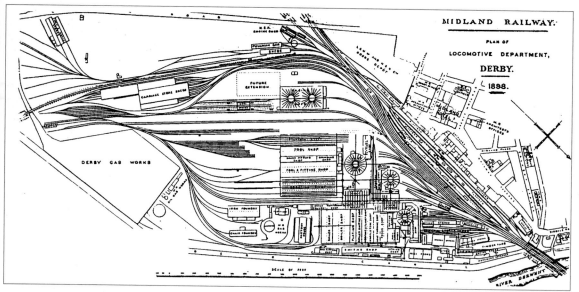

Locomotive department, Derby, 1898.

Behind the scenes at the Locomotive Works, *c*. 1910. (Author's Collection)

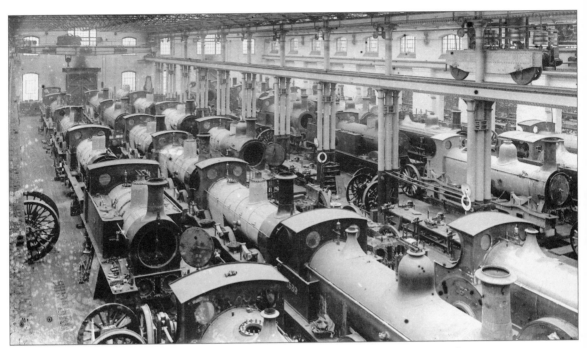

Two views of the Erecting Shop, Derby Locomotive Works, taken fifteen years apart. The top picture was taken in November 1895 and shows No. 8 Shop bursting at the seams with Kirtley and Johnson locomotives, including straight-framed goods engines and a couple of 0–4–4Ts. The bottom picture dates from July 1910. Improvements carried out include the installation of lights suspended from the roof supports and increased lifting capability owing to the fitting of additional travelling cranes. (Top picture NRM/DY802. Bottom picture NRM/DY9320)

Johnson's superbly engineered 4–2–2 No. 2601 *Princess of Wales* at Derby in December 1899 prior to being shipped to France for the 1900 Paris International Exhibition along with the GER's *Claude Hamilton* and the LNWR's *La France*. No. 2601, with her 7 ft 9½ in driving wheels, 19½ in × 26 in cylinders and double-bogie tender with its 4,000 gallon capacity, lifted the Grand Prix. This was a tribute to her excellent mechanical design and graceful appearance and to the skill of the craftsmen who constructed her. The prize was won in the face of adversity. Feelings were running high in Europe because of the South African War, a number of countries being sympathetic to the Boers. No. 2601 along with her sisters Nos 2602–2607 were to be the last Spinners built for the Midland, bringing the total constructed to ninety-five machines. (MR Official, Author's Collection)

During the late 1890s a dramatic upturn in freight traffic left the Midland and a number of other companies short of motive power. With locomotive manufacturers at full stretch and a well-timed engineering strike, the only alternative was to look overseas. The Government placed an order in the USA for one hundred 2–6–0s to be supplied in kit form. On arrival the locos were shared between the MR, GNR and GCR, Derby receiving thirty Baldwins and ten from Schenectady. The Baldwins were constructed in the open outside Derby Works. Apart from drawgear buffers, lamp brackets and coal rails on the tenders, Baldwin made no attempt to anglicize the design. The engines had 5 ft driving wheels, 18 in × 24 in cylinders and a working pressure of 160 psi. They were fitted with Coale pop safety valves, sported American chime whistles and had double-bogie tenders. One popular feature with footplate crews was the large cab, the roof of which extended back over the tender footplate. These stop-gap engines were all withdrawn by the end of 1915. (MR Official, Author's Collection)

Standing outside old No. 2 shed in March 1938 is newly built Stanier 2–6–4T No. 2431. Looking down the works yard the buildings are: to the left the Loco Stores (former NMR Engine Stores) and beyond that the Electric Shop, Coppersmiths and Brass Foundry; to the right are the Lagging Shop, Tender Shop and Erecting Shop. In the distance is the 35 ton travelling crane. Between 1923 and 1939 Derby Locomotive Works built a number of different locomotive types. As well as continuing to build 4F 0–6–0 goods engines, Derby turned out a further five batches of 4P 4–4–0 compounds commencing in February 1924 with Nos 1045–1064 (Order No. 5938). In September 1924 construction commenced on Nos 1065–1084 (Order No. 6066), to be followed by Nos 1085–1104 (Order No. 6293) and Nos 1105–1114 (Order No. 6354). In 1932 Nos 935–939 were built, the rest of the order for Nos 900–934 going to Vulcan Foundry. In December 1927 the works turned out No. 2300, the first of Henry Fowler's 2–6–4 passenger tank engines, followed by the LMS version of the Midland 2P and in 1930 by twenty Royal Scot class 4–6–0s, Nos 6150–6169. Though a small number of Jubilee class 4–6–0s and Stanier Black Fives were built, construction was orientated around tank engines and 4F 0–6–0s. In 1932 the works was involved in the LMS's first foray into diesel traction when an aging Johnson 0–6–0T No. 1831 was rebuilt into a shunting engine fitted with a six-cylinder Davey-Paxman 400 bhp diesel-hydraulic engine. Though this locomotive had a relatively short working life, it led to a series of trials using diesel shunting locomotives built by private manufacturers, and the construction at Derby of diesel-electric shunters Nos 7080–7119 between 1939 and 1942. (C.M. & J.M. Bentley)

Riddles standard design Class 5 mixed traffic 4–6–0 No. 73053 under construction during May 1953. The first of the class, No. 73000, had emerged from the works in April 1951, the first of 125 to be built at Derby. The last of the batch, No. 73154, was also the last steam locomotive to be built here, leaving the Erecting Shop on 14 June 1957. (C.M. & J.M. Bentley)

LMS 0–6–0 diesel electric shunter No. 7116 was one of a batch (Nos 7080–7119) built at Derby between 1939 and 1942. Fitted with an English Electric engine and transmission, the 350 bhp shunter had a maximum tractive effort of 33,500 lb and could go 20 mph flat out. Of the class, Nos 7100–7109 went directly to the WD as WD49–58. Others were loaned to the WD but Nos 7116–7119 always carried their LMS numbers. No. 7116 was allocated to Crewe South in March 1942, with a ten year spell at Willesden Junction before returning to Crewe in January 1955. By November 1956 she was at Speke Junction, being withdrawn in May 1966 and cut up at Derby a few months later. Under BR ownership she was renumbered No. 12029 on 7 September 1951. (NRM/DY28795)

Britain's first main line diesel electric locomotive, the 0–6–6–0 No. 10000, was completed at Derby in December 1947, a joint effort between the LMS and English Electric, who provided the four-stroke type 16SVT turbocharged V16 engine, type EE823A generator and EE519/1B force-ventilated 4 pole traction motors. The engine was rated at 1,600 bhp at 750 rpm, tractive effort being 41,400 lb maximum, 18,500 lb one hour rating and 15,000 lb continuous rating. In July 1948 sister engine No. 10001 was completed. The pair often worked coupled together and could be seen at Derby in the early evening, having worked in from London. No. 10000 was withdrawn in December 1963 and stored down the Klondyke. Here she languished until sold for scrap with an assortment of withdrawn steam locomotives and a number of other early diesels, including the former Southern trio 10201, 10202 and 10203. Also present were the diesel shunters 12011, 12022, ED2, ED4 and ED5. No. 10001 was withdrawn in March 1966 having completed around 1,000,000 miles in traffic. She was sold for scrap to Cox & Danks, Acton, London, in 1968. (LMS Official, DY35862)

No. D5000 was the first BR-designed diesel electric main line locomotive to be completed, and emerged from the works on 24 July 1958 resplendent in olive green paintwork and silver grey roof. Designed at Derby, the Type 2 (later Class 24) was rated at 1,160 bhp. Nos D5000–D5150 were constructed between July 1958 and April 1961. No. D5151 was the first of the 1,250 bhp models (later Class 25) and though she was built at Crewe, Derby went on to build Nos D5186–D5222, D5233–D5299, D7500–D7577, D7598–D7623 and D7660–D7677. And what of No. 5000? After going on show at Marylebone she was allocated to Crewe South. Withdrawn in January 1969 but reinstated to traffic the following October, she remained in service until July 1975, after which she was stored in serviceable condition. Officially withdrawn in January 1976 at Longsight, she was taken to Swindon and cut up in April 1977. Under the TOPS scheme No. D5000 became No. 24005 in November 1973. (Author's Collection)

No. 45009, seen here at the works, was an uprated version of Nos D1–D10 and was built at Derby in July 1961 as No. D37. Nos D11–D137 were equipped with the Sulzer 12LDA28–B engines delivering 2,500 bhp (1865 Kw) and Crompton Parkinson CP C172 A1 traction motors allowing a maximum speed of 90 mph. Redesignated Class 45 under the TOPS scheme, No. D37 became No. 45009 in December 1973. Withdrawn in September 1986, she was cut up at Vic Berry's yard, Leicester, in August 1988. (Tony Griffin)

No. 44005 *Cross Fell* being dismantled in the Erecting Shop. Designed in the Drawing Office of the CME (LMR) Derby, she was one of ten 2,300 bhp locomotives Nos D1–D10 built at the works between July 1959 and February 1960. Originally numbered No. D5, she became No. 44005 under the TOPS scheme in April 1974. On completion she was allocated to Camden (1B) along with her sisters Nos D2–D4 and Nos D6–D10. In March 1962 all ten Peaks were transferred to Toton (8A) and remained there until withdrawn. Under TOPS they became Class 44. Scrapping commenced in July 1976 with No. 44003 *Skiddaw*. No. 44005 was withdrawn in April 1978 and by the end of the year was nothing more than a memory. (Tony Griffin)

The former MR Way & Works Stores and the old Oil Stores photographed from London Road. In September 1961 a contract was placed with William Moss & Sons for the construction of a new engineering research centre to be built on the site. (BREL, Author's Collection)

The Railway Technical Centre shortly after completion. Officially opened on 14 May 1964 by HRH Prince Philip, the facility then comprised the Engineering Test Hall, laboratories and a five-storey administration block. Subsequent development of the site led in March 1967 to the opening of Trent House for use by the design staff from both the Locomotive Drawing Office and from the Carriage & Wagon Works. Also opened in March 1967 was Derwent House, which was the headquarters of BREL, the Central Purchasing Organization and the Staff & Services Section. Other buildings added to the complex included the Rolling Stock Development Unit Test Hall, the Advanced Projects Vehicles Laboratory, a technical library and so on. By 1972 it had become one of the most advanced technical centres in the world, capable of undertaking almost any type of railway-related research and development. At its height about 2,000 people were employed here but since the mid-1990s lack of investment and the run-up to privatization has brought about many redundancies. (BREL, Author's Collection)

Inside the Engineering Test Hall. Vehicles under test and evaluation include a unit from London Underground and a prototype LEV railbus. The box with the windows in it is the prototype Maglev vehicle which operated on a test track specially constructed for it. (BREL, Author's Collection)

Opened in 1970, the Advanced Projects Vehicles Laboratory covers 1,500 sq m. The photograph shows a Class 507 unit under test. In the background is the central control cabin from where scientists and engineers can monitor the progress of tests and experiments. (BREL, Author's Collection)

A development of the LEV railbus was the prototype Class 140 lightweight two-car DMU set, seen here at the Railway Technical Centre. Intended for branch line and local services, the Class 140 comprised two four-wheel units, DMS No. 55500 and DMS(L) No. 55501, each fitted with a Leyland 200 bhp (152 Kw) engine. Gangwayed throughout and fitted with folding doors, the units had a total seating capacity of 102. Each unit weighed 19 tonnes and had a maximum speed of 75 mph. Direct developments were Class 141 and Class 141/1, introduced in 1983 and 1988 respectively. (BREL, Author's Collection)

The prototype Maglev vehicle on test at the Research Centre (BREL, Author's Collection)

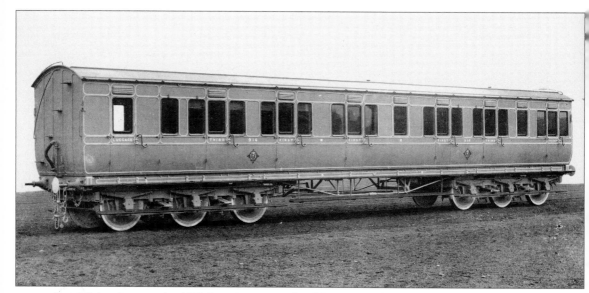

Grand Prix winner at the 1889 Paris International Exhibition was the Midland twelve-wheel pressed-steel-bodied composite coach designed by C&W Superintendent Thomas Clayton. The French judges were staggered by the fact that third-class passengers had lavatory access and soft seats. It was then still common practice for third-class coaches to have hard seats and third-class travellers strong bladders. (NRM/DY636)

The hydraulic lifting gear for hoisting coach bodies clear of their bogies, *c.* 1900. By 1898 the C&W employed 3,450 men, and weekly output ran at eight passenger coaches and 180 wagons. There were also 150 women employed in the upholsterers and sewing rooms, most of these being widows or relatives of railwaymen. (MR Official, Author's Collection)

Exhibitors unloading their wares at the showground sidings and platforms for the Royal Agricultural Show, June 1906. The showground covered 84 acres of the grounds of Osmaston Hall. The Midland are providing the cartage; there were stables at London Road and St Mary's Goods Yard. Access to the showground was through the C&W Works. In 1922 the MR still had 3,007 cart horses, 96 horses for shunting and 7,283 road vehicles on its books. The church on the left is St Osmund's, then only a couple of years old. (MR Official, Author's Collection)

The Midland Railway enquiry office situated at the Royal Showground, 1906, advertising the new service from Heysham to the Isle of Man and the north of Ireland (Author's Collection)

Works official photograph of brake 3rd No. 9933, 15 May 1935. Derby C&W Works remained busy throughout the inter-war period though work diversified in the late 1920s to include road vehicles, fitting bodies to single-deck Leyland buses and Morris and Karrier vans. Rolling stock output between the wars amounted to seven new carriages and anything up to 270 goods vehicles a week. From 1923 to the end of the Second World War the C&W built more than 76,000 wooden-bodied goods vehicles, including 62,000 mineral wagons. (NRM/DY19987)

Like all major railway workshops in the Second World War, Derby played a full part in contributing towards the war effort. Work undertaken included the production of 17- and 25-pdr field guns, tank turrets, bomb casings and Bailey bridge panels. The picture shows 12 in rail-mounted howitzers in the C&W yard. Repair work was carried out on the fuselage sections of Whitley, Lancaster and Hampden bombers and fighter aircraft wing assemblies. Railway work included a shared order with Wolverton to supply sixty-six trains for military use at home and overseas. Derby also built the prototype CAM catapult, a stopgap measure until sufficient aircraft carriers were operational, which gave merchant ships limited air cover mid-Atlantic by launching a Hurricane fighter. The only problem was that when launched the Hurricane had no means of landing back aboard ship, the pilot having to ditch and hope someone would pick him up. (Author's Collection)

Blackout curtains are fitted to a restaurant car. War timetables had been prepared by the LMS in July 1939, coming into force on Monday 11 September. Dining and sleeping car services were suspended, though eventually reinstated. However, in order to increase carrying capacity and discourage all but essential rail travel only twenty-eight dining cars were in service after May 1942 and these too were withdrawn from April 1944. A limited dining car service was reintroduced during 1945. (Author's Collection)

Derby-built lightweight two-car DMU set on trials, c. 1955. No. E79614 was one of the vehicles in the series Nos M79600–E79625 and Nos M79639–M79684. Eastern Region sets seated 32 first- and 106 second-class passengers. One unit, No. M79649 (later Departmental No. DB999510), was fitted out as an inspection saloon, complete with pantry, and was not in public service. (Author's Collection)

The prototype HST diesel electric power car No. 252001 with its distinctive driving cab at the C&W Works. The prototype set consisted of seven Mk III coaches sandwiched between two power cars. Evaluation trials commenced during 1972 and on 11 June 1973 the HST reached 143 mph between Darlington and York. In the spring of 1977 the first production sets went into revenue earning service on the Western Region's Paddington–Bristol/South Wales routes. (Tony Griffin)

The prototype APTP at the C&W Works, August 1978. Mounted on articulated bogies, the full formation in service as planned was a driving trailer, a second-class intermediate trailer, a second-class/catering trailer, an unclassified trailer for catering service, a van trailer with seating for first-class passengers and two pantograph power units in the centre. The rear half of the train would then duplicate the front portion but in reverse order. Because the driving compartments were separate the power cars could be built to develop 5,500 bhp without exceeding the weight restriction of 69 tonnes. (Tony Griffin)

THE LINE TO MANCHESTER

Coming off the curve to Chaddesden this grubby looking Austerity 2–8–0 is about to rattle past photographer Chris Canner, trundle over Five Arches bridge and on through the station. Built in large numbers from 1943, no fewer than 733 of these Riddles-designed locomotives were taken into BR stock as Nos 90000–90732. Withdrawn between 1959 and 1967, not one survived into preservation. However, the K&WVR are in the process of constructing one out of bits and pieces from around Europe, which will carry the number 90733. (Chris Canner)

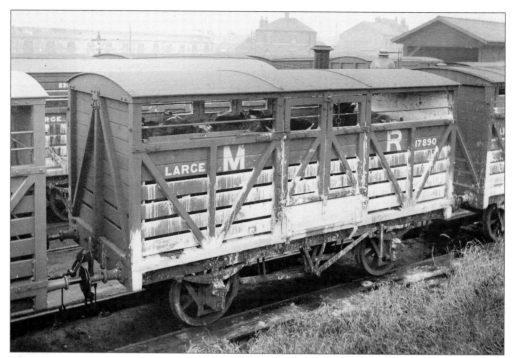

Situated just north of the station near to the signal works was the cattle dock. The long single-storey building in the background is the slaughterhouse which stood on the opposite bank of the River Derwent. The long line of doors are the individual slaughtering pens. Having been brought up on Siddals Road just a couple of hundred yards away, I can tell you that there were times when the smell from the slaughterhouse and adjacent tannery really was something else! (NRM/DY9165)

The first station out of Derby was Nottingham Road, opened in 1856 in connection with the Ripley branch. The station soon proved so popular with passengers because of its close proximity to the town centre that the platforms had to be extended and a waiting shed built. The station was only a few minutes walk away from Derby Racecourse and therefore extra busy on race days, not only with punters but also with horses. It was used to unload the horses for Buffalo Bill's Wild West Show when it visited Derby. Even in the late 1950s the horse dock was used to offload circus animals whenever the big top came to town. The picture shows the station decorated for the Royal Show in 1906. Nottingham Road closed on 6 March 1967. (M.L. Knighton Collection)

The Derby breakdown train in action at Breadsall Crossing in 1906, with the 15 ton Cowans Sheldon steam crane about to drag Kirtley 700 Class 0–6–0 No. 1045 out of the hole it had dug for itself after becoming derailed. Built by Dubs & Co. in 1873, the 0–6–0 was renumbered No. 2847 in 1907. She was one of thirty-one Kirtley class 2 double-framers to survive into LMS ownership and was withdrawn in December 1933. (M.L. Knighton Collection)

Heading towards Derby on the Up goods, a special coal train passes milepost 130 on the Derby–Leeds line in February 1940. (Author's Collection)

Duffield in the Midland era. The top picture dates from between about 1904 and 1910, when the signal gantry was erected and Duffield station signalbox demolished. In February 1910 the signalling for the station was rationalized, all functions being carried out from the box at Duffield Junction where a new thirty-six lever frame had been installed. In the bottom picture station staff demonstrate that neatness and cleanliness were the order of the day. (Author's Collection)

Duffield station, in a view looking north, 25 August 1952. The main station building is on the platform to the left. In 1969 Duffield was reduced to an unmanned halt and by the end of the year semaphores had given way to colour lights, the signalbox had closed and the Up waiting room, main building, branch line waiting room, even the bike shed had all been demolished. (LGRP)

Belper, in a view looking in the Down direction, August 1952. (Author's Collection)

The NMR station at Amber Gate, built in 1839 to a design by architect Francis Thompson. Designed in the Jacobean style, it was renamed Ambergate in November 1846. In 1863 the station was dismantled, moved about 450 yd south and rebuilt brick by brick. Closed to passengers in December 1876 when the famous triangular station was commissioned, it was demolished in what can only be described as an act of vandalism by BR. (Author's Collection)

The scene following a collision between two goods trains at Ambergate South Junction, 3 March 1888. Apparently a Manchester–Leicester train had collided with a Derby–York service while the latter was engaged in a shunt. (M.L. Knighton Collection)

Ambergate, in a view looking south-east from the Crich mineral railway, 20 April 1911. This excellent photograph shows off the station's triangular layout. In the near platform is thought to be a train bound for Pye Bridge, while on the far side is an Up express heading for Derby. The lines to and from Manchester are on the right-hand side of the picture. (NRM/DY9491)

Ambergate's wooden buildings caught fire on several occasions, sometimes with spectacular results. This particular event is thought to have occurred during the First World War. (M.L. Knighton Collection)

Platform 2, 1 September 1953. In the background one of the station staff tinkers with his motorcycle, shirt sleeves rolled up. This interesting picture has lots of detail for the modeller. (BR Official, M.L. Knighton Collection)

Bursting out of the 764 yd long Willersley Tunnel and into the sunlight, Black Five No. 45279 thunders through Cromford on 24 May 1952. One of the more fascinating accounts of Cromford with its chateau-inspired station has been left by children's writer Alison Uttley. Growing up at Castle Top Farm in the early years of this century, Alison went to school by train. She would catch the 0750 hrs, which had reserved carriages for the girls attending grammar school. The guard, who wore a buttonhole all through the spring, summer and autumn, would check on the girls' safety at every stop. Alison went on to tell how she lost her school hat; it blew off one morning when she lent out of a carriage window. The result was her being paraded before the entire school and reprimanded for 'bad behaviour on the train', and for failing to behave with the decorum expected of a person travelling upon the Midland Railway. (C.M & J.M. Bentley)

Matlock Bath was heavily promoted as a tourist town by the Midland in its advertising literature. The railway promoted its route to Manchester as the best for comfortable travel and picturesque scenery. Both these photographs were taken in 1908. (F.W. Stevenson, courtesy J.D. Whitworth)

Matlock Bath station, 1890s. In keeping with the surrounding countryside the station was designed and built in a Swiss chalet style. Though the signalbox and goods shed are just a memory, much of the main building survives and is owned by Derbyshire Dales District Council. Visitors to Matlock Bath can now park on what was the station forecourt and goods yard. (Author's Collection)

Jubilee No. 5654 *Hood* pulls out of Matlock with a south-bound express, 20 July 1946. The unusual elevated signalbox dated from 1910 when it replaced two smaller boxes. This eccentric construction spanned the line to the goods shed, the signalman having to clamber up steep steps to gain access. The goods shed is still extant (1997) though in a dilapidated condition. (J.D. Whitworth)

Matlock was in much reduced circumstances when this photograph was taken. Through trains to Manchester were a thing of the past and Matlock had been reduced to one platform. 'The Choppers' were on a round trip from Derby to Matlock and back as part of a RPPR railtour on 18 March 1978. (Tony Griffin)

Peak Rail, a preservation project dedicated to restoring the former Midland line between Matlock and Buxton, operates over 4 miles of the old route from Matlock Riverside (just beyond the old goods shed) to Rowsley South. One of the mainstays of Peak Rail's motive power has been 0–6–0ST *Warrington*, built by Robert Stephenson & Hawthorns in 1944 (works number 7136). (B. Blood)

Though primarily designed for heavy freight trains, 9Fs were sometimes called upon to work passenger turns to express timings. Seen here at Peak Rail's Darley Dale station is the East Somerset Railway's preserved engine No. 92203 *Black Prince* about to set off on the 2 mile trip to Matlock Riverside. (B. Blood)

Type 4 1Co-Co1 No. D8 *Penyghent* is now based at Peak Rail, Matlock, following her withdrawal from BR. On 29 March 1997, Easter Sunday, *Penyghent* top and tailed a train with preserved Black Five No. M5337 for a special train marking the opening of Peak Rail's 2 mile extension from Darley Dale to Rowsley South. The reason for the top and tailing is that the run-round loop at Matlock Riverside is too short to facilitate a train of this length. (Tony Griffin)

Rowsley South for the time being is the northern terminus of Peak Rail's line from Matlock Riverside. Opened on 29 March 1997 the station is well built if somewhat spartan from an architectural point of view. Rowsley does, however, have masses of car parking space, so pay a visit and give support to this marvellous project to reinstate the Midland main line to the north-west. (Author's Collection)

The old station at Rowsley, 8 August 1953. Rowsley was the northern end of the grandly titled Manchester, Buxton, Matlock & Midlands Junction Railway, though the only section to be built was between Ambergate and Rowsley. Opened in 1848, the MBM&MJR was leased jointly by the LNWR and the Midland. When the Midland who operated the line commenced construction of its extension toward Buxton, a realignment of the route resulted in a new passenger station being built. The new station opened in August 1862; the old one was then relegated to a goods depot in which function it served for many years. Reputedly designed by Sir Joseph Paxton, the old station still exists. The site was occupied by the Hinckley Group but is now (1997) vacant and available for leasing. (C.M. & J.M. Bentley)

Pre-nationalization days at Rowsley. Jinty 0–6–0T No. 7460 and former Midland 1F 0–6–0T No. 1875 are both engaged in a spot of shunting. (M.L. Knighton Collection)

In the Derby Glass Plate Register the first 251 photographs have nothing whatsoever to do with engines, carriages, stations or signals. They were taken at the behest of the Advertising Department keen to promote the tourist angle. In June 1885 the official photographer visited Cromford and Bonsall; there were regular visits to Matlock, Bakewell, Buxton and Ashford-in-the-Water. Haddon Hall was photographed in April 1893 and again in April 1896. The pictures were used to produce a series of postcards entitled 'Midland Route, the best route for comfortable travel and picturesque scenery'. (Author's Collection)

Bakewell station, looking toward Derby, 30 September 1903. Bakewell conformed to the distinctive style created by architect Edward Walters of a long single-storey structure, tall chimney-stacks and iron and glass canopies over the platforms. Bakewell closed to passenger traffic on 6 March 1967 and to goods traffic on 1 July 1968. (NRM/DY2461)

Stanier 8F No. 48369 clears Bakewell on a Buxton–Chaddesden Sidings freight, 18 May 1966. (C.M. & J.M. Bentley)

Great Longstone (for Ashford) was originally called Longstone. Designed by Edward Walters, the station was an ornate version of Great Glen on the Leicester–Hitchin line. Peak Forest station was very similar. Great Longstone closed on 10 September 1962. The photograph dates from 1933 and depicts LMS Compound No. 1021 on a stopping train. This engine was built in April 1906 as No. 1016 and renumbered in 1907. Rebuilt in 1927 with a G9AS superheated boiler she survived into BR days and was withdrawn in October 1952. (C.M. & J.M. Bentley)

Printed in Saxony, this chromotype postcard of Monsal Dale viaduct was on sale before the First World War. The curve in the viaduct can be seen; the portal of Headstone Tunnel (533 yd) is on the left. (Author's Collection)

'The Arcadia of Derbyshire' was the title once attributed to Monsal Dale. Spectacular scenery complemented by the meandering River Wye makes the area a favourite with walkers to this day. In this picture taken in about 1912 a Down goods trundles over the viaduct heading north. (C.M. & J.M. Bentley)

Monsal Dale station was originally intended to be for goods traffic only, serving Cressbrook Mill, which is situated in the valley below. However, a change in policy resulted in the minimalist passenger station opening for business on 1 September 1866. Built out of second-hand materials, the wooden station building came from Evesham, the Down platform was built of stone and the Up was made of timber, and the whole lot cost less than £100. But in the early years of its existence Monsal Dale wasn't the place to be after a few beers and a good curry; the toilets weren't added until 1875. The single goods siding served, among others, the Monsal Dale Spar Mine. The station was closed to goods traffic on 27 August 1966 and completely on 6 March 1967. (Author's Collection)

Kirtley 1070 Class 2–4–0 No. 1088, completed in 1875 and photographed at what is thought to be Millers Dale. This was Kirtley's last design though the locomotives themselves weren't built until after his death. (Author's Collection)

4F No. 43945 struts its stuff across the old (1863) viaduct and on through Millers Dale. In the background are the remains of the defunct Millers Dale Lime Co. (C.M. & J.M. Bentley)

At 1105 hrs on a bleak snowswept winter's morning the 1025 hrs ex-Manchester Central–London service pulls into Millers Dale, 23 January 1965. At nearly 800 ft above sea level, this imposing station boasted five platforms as well as the local post office, which was situated at the 'town' end of platform 1. (B. Blood)

2P No. 482 pilots Black Five No. 5278 through Millers Dale Junction with a Manchester-bound express. The lines to the right lead to and from Buxton, which for many years was linked to Millers Dale by means of a push-and-pull passenger service hauled by 0–4–4Ts. (C.M. & J.M. Bentley)

An unidentified Stanier 8F pushes hard as it assists a stone train up the 1 in 90 main line towards Great Rocks. The photographs were taken from the ICI Tunstead side of the boundary fence. (B. Blood)

4F 0–6–0 No. 44214 leads Stanier 8F No. 48627 in a spirited assault up the gradient from Tunstead to Peak Forest, 8 August 1964. Part of the ICI works can be seen in the background. (C.M. & J.M. Bentley)

History in the making, 26 April 1994. Driver Baz Blood waits for the signalman at Great Rocks to pull off for the first 6E56 Tunstead–Drax working to be hauled by a National Power-owned Class 59 locomotive. At that time No. 59201 *Vale of York* was the only Class 59 owned by National Power though others have since been acquired. The initial work pattern for No. 59201 was that it would work to Tunstead early on a Monday morning after spending the weekend at National Power's maintenance facility. It would then in effect be based at Peak Forest until the following Friday, when after unloading at Drax it would again go to the service facility and remain there until the following Monday when the pattern would be repeated. (B. Blood)

Reliving days gone by. Carnforth-based preserved 8F No. 48151 reverses towards Causeway Tunnel in BLI Tunstead. The 8F was stabled here for a few days as part of the celebrations commemorating the sixtieth anniversary of the Tunstead hopper trains. (B. Blood)

Britannia Class 4–6–2 No. 70021 *Morning Star* thunders up the gradient at Great Rocks with a Manchester express. The Britannias were the first BR standard design to be introduced, a total of fifty-five being built between 1951 and 1954. Of these, No. 70000 *Britannia* and No. 70013 *Oliver Cromwell* have been preserved. (C.M. & J.M. Bentley)

Stanier 8F No. 48605 about to go for a spin on the turntable at Great Rocks to the accompaniment of much groaning and not a little swearing from her traincrew. A grand total of 852 8Fs were built between 1935 and 1946, No. 48605 being constructed by the Southern Railway. The turntable pit still exists and every year it fills up with water from the surrounding high ground, overflowing on to the track under the road bridge where it floods the Down line, then on past Great Rocks box. Several years ago, one of the area freight managers suggested that the flooding could be solved by dynamiting the pit to crack open its base. When it was pointed out that because of the geology of the immediate area it could make matters worse the idea was quietly dropped. (C.M & J.M. Bentley)

Looking down the gradient towards Great Rocks. In the foreground are the engine holding sidings at Peak Forest. When the line was open throughout, Peak Forest Summit marked the end of a gruelling 15 miles for Manchester-bound traffic, much of it at 1 in 90 and 1 in 100. (Chris Law)

On 9 February 1957 driver John Axon was working a Buxton–Arpley unfitted freight with Stanier 8F No. 48188. On the journey to Buxton, Axon had experienced some problems with steam escaping from the steam brake handle. A fitter tightened up a loose nut which appeared to cure the problem, but on the return trip steam again began escaping. Axon decided to make for Bibbington's Sidings from where he could send for help. However, before he could do this the pipe union blew apart releasing scalding steam into the cab and forcing Axon and his fireman back to the tender. It was now impossible to make a full brake application or sound the whistle, and to make matters even worse the train was being banked by another 8F which was pushing for all its worth, the crew oblivious to Axon's plight. While Axon attempted to regain control of his engine, the fireman jumped off and attempted to drop as many brakes as he could on the thirty-four vehicle train. Though some brakes were dropped, the train was moving too fast and on clearing the summit it accelerated away down the incline. The signalman at Dove Holes was placed in an invidious position. He could put Axon's train into the loop and let it crash there, or he could let it run. He chose the latter in the hope that Axon would regain control and then warned Chapel-en-le-Frith Central that they had a runaway heading towards them. Station staff at Chapel lost no time in evacuating a two-car DMU in the Up platform but it was already too late to warn the crew of the Down Rowsley–Stockport goods. No. 48188 smashed into the rear of the goods killing its guard and John Axon in the process. Despite having the opportunity to jump clear, John Axon chose to remain with his engine and attempt to regain control. His courage was recognized by the posthumous award of the George Cross, the highest honour for bravery beyond the call of duty that can be bestowed upon a citizen of the UK. (C.M. & J.M. Bentley)

Standard Class 5 mixed traffic 4–6–0 No. 73001 pulls out of Chapel-en-le-Frith Central with an Up stopping passenger train. Designed by Edward Walters, the station opened on 2 February 1867 as Chapel-en-le-Frith. On 2 June 1924 the station was renamed Chapel-en-le-Frith Central, the station on the former LNWR line between Buxton and Stockport becoming Chapel-en-le-Frith South. Central lost its goods traffic on 2 December 1963 and closed completely on 6 March 1967. Also in the picture is the station's Midlands-style period III signalbox which opened in June 1905, replacing two earlier boxes. The main station building still exists. One of the more interesting proposals under privatization was one to operate a one-way circular passenger service from Manchester. The trains would leave Piccadilly and run to a new station at Buxton via the old LNWR line. The return journey would be via Great Rocks, Peak Forest and Chinley. The proposal included the closure of the Chapel station on the LNWR line in favour of a new one on the old Midland. (C.M. & J.M. Bentley)

Class 45 No. 45041 *Royal Tank Regiment* at Chinley North Junction, 9 February 1980. Introduced in June 1962 as No. D53, this locomotive was initially allocated to Derby. It was named in June 1964 and became No. 45041 in May 1975. Its final allocation was Tinsley from where it was withdrawn from service in May 1988. This locomotive is now at the Midland Railway Centre, Butterley. (Author's Collection)

SECTION THREE

AROUND BUXTON

With a good head of steam Black Five No. 45139 rounds the curve at Blackwell Mill with a Buxton–Manchester service. (C.M. & J.M. Bentley)

Tarmac Roadstone show off their new wagons built for working out of Topley Pike. Until a few years ago a Limestone Supertrain was operated as a joint venture between Tarmac and Peakstone, the usual consisting of thirty-eight PGAs carrying a total of 1,400 tons. In the top picture, driver Charlie Meade, in command of Class 40 No. 40114, poses for the camera, the train being positioned on the Topley Pike headshunt. It is thought that No. 40114, was only buffered up to the wagons for the benefit of the photographer as her air brake system wasn't connected up. In the lower picture, driver Chris Elvidge has moved the rake to Blackwell Mill where a series of photographs were taken. Chris has brought his Class 47 No. 47230 to a stand on Blackwell Mill curve opposite the site where Peak Forest Junction signalbox once stood. The rubble behind the train is the debris left following the demolition of Buxton Central Lime Works. (Chris Elvidge Collection)

Stanier two-cylinder superheated 2–6–4T No. 42543 on an Up Uttoxeter at Higher Buxton on a snow dusted morning in February 1953. No. 42543 was one of a class of 206 engines built between 1935 and 1943. Nos 42537–42544 originally had domeless boilers, although one or two of the later engines had domes. All 206 were withdrawn between 1961 and 1967. (C.M. & B.M. Bentley)

Class 37 No. 37415 *Highland Region* at the head of a return working of 7T81 Tunstead–Hindlow ore train awaits in Buxton URS for a path to Great Rocks. This was the first revenue-earning run for this locomotive following its transfer to Buxton in March 1993. (B. Blood)

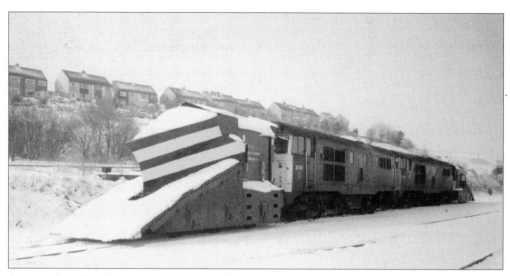

Awaiting the call to duty in Buxton URS are the depot's snowploughs and a pair of Class 31s. When a severe snow warning was received, Buxton always got the ploughs ready for action. I remember in February 1991 being on the night turn at Great Rocks box when it snowed heavily. The ploughs were out, and with the help of the lads from our local track gang we managed to move locos and hoppers so that both Tunstead and Peak Forest had trains ready to roll. Chaos reigned at Chinley and beyond, however, with the result that nothing ran. (B. Blood)

The first 9F to be allocated to Buxton seen shortly after her arrival. The 9F was probably the best heavy freight steam locomotive to run on BR and would have given excellent service well beyond 1968. The original BR standard heavy freight design was for a 2–8–2 but the fact that there were a large number of former WD and other goods engines in service delayed the project. (B. Blood)

One of a class of 192 superheated goods engines designed by Henry Fowler and introduced from October 1911, 4F 0–6–0 No. 43967 is seen at Buxton shortly before the end of her career, painted with the yellow diagonal stripe to indicate that she was forbidden to work south of Crewe under electrified lines. This highly successful design was more powerful than Deeley's standard goods engine introduced in 1906. A further 580 4Fs were built by the LMS, including four for the S&DJR. (B. Blood)

Buxton in the late 1970s, with a two-car lightweight DMU set on the Manchester Piccadilly service via the LNWR line to Stockport. The window at the end of the platform is virtually the only reminder of the LNWR trainshed that once graced the station. Superbly designed, the Midland station was its twin; the trainshed was a godsend during the Buxton winters. (Tony Griffin)

Leaving Peak Rail's Buxton site for pastures new is Hunslet 0–6–0ST *Brookes No. 1* (HE 2387/1941). This engine had been purchased for a preservation scheme on the Delph branch which unfortunately came to little, though a few track panels were laid. *Brookes No. 1* is now a resident on the Middleton Railway, Leeds. (B. Blood)

Preserved 8F No. 48624 undergoing restoration at Peak Rail, Buxton. The engine is parked alongside the former Midland goods shed which housed the society's gift shop and museum. The site was eventually sold to Buxton Mineral Water, Peak Rail decamping lock, stock and locos to Darley Dale. The goods shed was demolished in April 1997. (B. Blood)

ALONG THE HOPE VALLEY

Chinley, 25 February 1903. Work is still in progress on the new enlarged station, built 440 yd west of the original. The new station had five through platforms and a bay; there were also enlarged goods handling facilities and provision was made for the watering and turning of locomotives. One of the features of this station was its distinctive footbridge, which spanned all six platforms as well as the two loop lines. The picture was taken at the South Junction looking in the direction of Manchester. The economic boom of the 1890s brought with it the country's final bout of railway construction. The Midland's contribution was the construction of its link between Manchester and Sheffield, authorization being granted in 1888. The Dore & Chinley line was to run from a junction at Dore, through Totley Tunnel, which when built would be 3 miles 950 yd in length (the second longest main line tunnel in the British Isles), thence along the Hope Valley and on through the Vale of Edale to Chinley, where it would join the route from Derby to Manchester. The line opened for goods traffic on 6 November 1893, giving the Midland an opportunity to compete against the MS&L's Woodhead route. (NRM/DY2470)

Chinley Station North Junction. Black Five No. 5342 pulls away from platform 2, and takes the Down Slow to the Down Fast, 29 May 1938. (C.M. & B.M. Bentley)

One of Ivatt's class 2 light 2–6–0s No. 46465 at Chinley on 9 June 1964 working the 0939 hrs Sheffield–Chinley–Sheffield service. Built by the LMS and BR, these superb machines were superseded in some areas by the similar standard class 2 Nos 78000–78064. A number have been preserved including Nos 6441, 46443, 46447, 46464, 46512 and 46521. (C.M. & J.M. Bentley)

A directors' inspection train to the east of Cowburn Tunnel, 10 August 1893. The train is hauled by the venerable 0–4–2ST Cockermouth, formerly of the Cockermouth & Workington Railway and later the LNWR, who sold her out of service to the contractor T. Oliver. One of the dignitaries is thought to be Samuel Johnson (seated at extreme left). (NRM/DY1968)

Compound No. 41072 sprints out of Cowburn Tunnel with a rake of blood and custard liveried coaches. The engine still sports her LMS logo on the tender but carries her BR number. Built at Derby in 1924, No. 41078 was withdrawn in March 1958. (C.M. & B.M. Bentley)

Earles Sidings, serving Blue Circle Cement. Blue liveried split-headcode Class 37 No. 37083 heads west out of the yard. This EE Type 3 was introduced in December 1962, one of a batch built by RSH and carrying the BR number No. D6783. She was renumbered No. 37083 in March 1974. By 1997 she was in store at Doncaster awaiting a decision on her future. (B. Blood)

H-boilered 0–6–0 No. 3728 trundles through Hathersage with a banana train, 31 July 1911. (NRM/DY9588)

A 9F heads through Hathersage, the supposed last resting place of Robin Hood's sidekick Little John. The station closed to goods traffic on 30 January 1965, becoming an unstaffed halt on 7 September 1969. (Author's Collection)

EASTER RAIL CRUISE IN DERBYSHIRE

CHEAP TRIP

BY

DIESEL TRAIN

HATHERSAGE

Sunday 14th April 1963

FROM	TIMES OF DEPARTURE	RETURN FARES Second Class	ARRIVAL TIMES ON RETURN
	pm	s d	pm
NOTTINGHAM Midland ...	2 30	8/3	8 43
BEESTON...	2 38		8 34
TRENT	2 45		8 24
SAWLEY JUNCTION ...	2 50		8 18
DRAYCOTT & BREASTON ...	2 55	7/6	8 14
BORROWASH	3 1		8 8
SPONDON	3 5		8 4
DERBY Midland ...	3 15	7/3	7 55
BELPER	3 29	5/6	7 43
AMBERGATE	3 35	5/3	7 36
HATHERSAGE ... ... arrive	pm 5 20	Passengers return same day at ...	pm 6 55

The train will proceed on the outward journey through the beautiful Derbyshire dales via Matlock, Bakewell and Miller's Dale and thence through the Hope Valley to Hathersage allowing approximately 1¼ hours' stay at that point. The return journey will be made via Grindleford, Chesterfield and Wingfield.

Children under 3 years of age, free; 3 years and under 14, half-fares (fractions of a 1d. reckoned as a 1d.).

Rail tickets can be obtained in advance at stations and official railway agents

Further information will be supplied on application to stations, official railway agents, or to Commercial Manager, Alan House, Clumber Street, Nottingham. Telephone 48531, Extn. 40.

LONDON MIDLAND   *Travel in Rail Comfort*   March 1963   BR 35000

Arthur Gaunt & Sons (Printers) Ltd., Hanover, Derbyshire.

LMS 2P enters Totley Tunnel, the second longest in the UK at 3 miles 950 yd. To the west is Cowburn Tunnel, ranked ninth with a length of 2 miles 182 yd. (Author's Collection)

Grindleford, when the wooden station building containing the ticket office and stationmaster's living quarters was still under construction, *c.* 1900. Grindleford remains open and is a popular destination for walkers and cyclists. The station building is now a café. (Author's Collection)

Grindleford signalbox and frame, April 1997. (Author's Collection)

The twisted spire of St Mary's leaves one in no doubt that this is Chesterfield. The photograph dates from August 1888 and shows the MR station that opened in May 1870. (Author's Collection)

The last grand scheme of the 1890s in Derbyshire was the construction of the Lancashire, Derbyshire & East Coast Railway. The LD&ECR Bill went before Parliament in 1891 facing opposition from the LNWR, the Midland, the MS&L, the Cheshire Lines Committee and the Great Northern & Great Eastern Joint; all except the MR and the MS&LR eventually withdrew. The LD&ECR intended to construct a main line from Warrington to Sutton-on-Sea together with a number of branch lines connecting either with other railways or serving collieries. Indeed, the whole purpose of the line was to serve the rich and still expanding coalfield of Nottinghamshire and Derbyshire; the original list of promoters was almost a who's who of local coal or landowners. The company was authorized to raise £5,000,000 with a further £1,300,000 in borrowing powers. In June 1892 work began on the central section from Chesterfield to a junction with the GN&GEJt at Pyewipe near Lincoln. The GER had changed tack, no longer opposing the line but actively supporting it to the tune of £250,000 worth of shares and a director on the board. Lack of subscriptions to the share issue left the LD&ECR in a very weak position, giving the GER tremendous influence on the course of events. Matters came to a head in February 1894 when the contractors refused shares instead of money. The LD&ECR had no alternative but to go to the GER for financial assistance. The GER offered £250,000 of capital but only if plans to build the line to the west of Chesterfield were abandoned and the proposed section to the east of Lincoln transferred to a separate company. Despite problems with Bolsover Tunnel, the official opening took place on 8 March 1897 giving Chesterfield its third railway station. The LD&ECR's principal engineering feats were the 700 ft long Chesterfield Viaduct which carried the railway over the River Hipper, the Midland main line between Sheffield and Derby, and the MS&L's Chesterfield Loop Line. The following year the LD&ECR branch between Langwith Junction and Beighton opened, and the MS&L's London Extension in 1899. The company had prospered under the chairmanship of Sir Edward Watkin. He had fought to secure parliamentary approval for the MS&L to construct an independent line to the capital. When permission was at last given, Watkin proudly changed the company name to the Great Central Railway.

The Edwardian era brought with it a sharp decline in railway construction. A few branch lines were built and agreements on running powers reached, but for the most part companies got on with vying with one another for traffic; the more affluent and influential engaged in a bout of amalgamations and takeovers. In 1899 the MR absorbed the Barnoldswick Railway, followed in 1912 by the London Tilbury & Southend and in 1914 by the Tottenham & Forest Gate. In 1907 it was the turn of the LD&ECR, which, under Harry Wilmot, had built up its freight traffic from four trains each way daily in 1896 to seventy-five a day not including branch line workings. However, abandonment of the original proposals had left it as little more than a feeder line for other companies and absorption was always only a question of time. Both the GNR and GCR expressed interest; the GER didn't need to as it already had running powers which would remain whoever acquired it. In the end, it was the GCR.

AROUND CHESTERFIELD

Designed in the Jacobean style by NRM architect Francis Thompson, Chesterfield was the largest intermediate station between Derby and Leeds for a number of years. This station survived until May 1870 when it was superseded by a new one approximately 100 yd further north. The elegant building in the background with the columnar chimney is a pump house and a water supply tank for locomotives. (Author's Collection)

The exterior of Chesterfield Midland, as depicted in Nadins series of local postcards. (Author's Collection)

Staveley allocated 3F 0–6–0 No. 43299 shunting at Chesterfield, 10 June 1950. This engine was one of 387 3Fs to pass into BR ownership and was a rebuild of a Johnson 2F. She was fitted with a non-superheated Belpaire boiler with a working pressure of 175 psi, 18 in × 26 in inside cylinders and 5 ft 3 in driving wheels. Over 200 3Fs were still active in the early 1960s but by 1963 this had been reduced to just three, Nos 43620, 43637 and 43669, all allocated to Derby. I once saw No. 43669 trundle over Five Arches bridge at Derby with her connecting rods missing making her a 2–2–2. Though none survived into preservation, the Midland Railway Centre, Butterley, did propose converting a Jinty 0–6–0T into a replica 3F. (C.M. & J.M. Bentley)

Hasland 2P 4–4–0 No. 40370 at Chesterfield, 10 June 1950. This was one of seventeen veterans of a series of 4–4–0s built between 1882 and 1891 to be absorbed into BR stock, and numbered 40332–40397. Of these, Nos 40383, 40385 and 40391 were non-superheated. The large crane in the background is in the yard at Markham Engineering, which had an internal railway system not connected to the main line. (C.M. & J.M. Bentley)

Black Five No. 44928 draws into Chesterfield with a Derby-bound express, 10 June 1950. Though carrying her BR smokebox numberplate, No. 44928's tender still bears the LMS legend. (C.M. & J.M. Bentley)

Thirty-four years separates this picture of Class 37 No. 37174 and that of No. 44928 on p. 81. During the intervening years Chesterfield has changed: new lighting, colour light signals and the closure of the mechanical signalbox. Only the fencing remains the same. (Chris Law)

Seen here in a scrapyard at Chesterfield in 1961 is Black Hawthorn 0–6–0ST *Isaac Limb*. Built in about 1874, this engine is thought to have been supplied new to a contractor before being purchased for use at Staveley Ironworks. At some time in its career the cab had been rebuilt. (Vic Hall)

Chesterfield, 10 June 1950. Black Five No. 44817 coasts effortlessly past LMS-liveried 4F No. 3991. A few minutes later, Stanier 8F No. 48271 appeared on the scene. (C.M. & J.M. Bentley)

The former LD&ECR terminus was situated at West Bars near to the market-place. There were four platforms, extensive goods facilities and a small locomotive depot. The platforms appear to have been numbered on the American track system as there were platforms 1, 2, 4 and 5 but no No. 3, this being the engine release road for platforms (tracks) 2 and 4. When the GCR took over this station it was renamed Chesterfield Market Place. It closed to passengers on 3 December 1951 and completely on 4 March 1957. (Author's Collection)

The GCR station was renamed Chesterfield Central on 1 January 1907 following the GCR takeover of the LD&ECR. When the takeover was first announced there were no direct connections between GCR and LD&ECR metals, though this was remedied by 1907. Central closed to passengers on 4 March 1963 and completely on 11 September 1967. (Author's Collection)

Scarcliffe was on the Chesterfield–Langwith Junction section of the LD&ECR. The LD&ECR was never very hot on passenger trains; its business was moving goods and mineral traffic of which there were seventy-five trains a day in each direction by 1906. This picture, taken in 1911, shows the stationmaster and his family. At this time Scarcliffe's weekday passenger service consisted of just four trains a day in each direction. (Author's Collection)

Given its size, Langwith Junction's passenger services in 1911 were little better than Scarcliffe's, with four in each direction to Chesterfield and five to Sheffield. Renamed Shirebrook North on 2 June 1924, the station lost its passenger services on 19 September 1955, though summer Saturday and bank holiday specials to Boston and Skegness continued to pick up and set down. These services finally ceased on 5 September 1965, goods traffic finishing ten years later. (Author's Collection)

Pilsley on the GCR line between Chesterfield and Nottingham, photographed for this postcard just a year or so before the outbreak of the First World War. This small but pleasant-looking station closed completely on 2 November 1959. (Author's Collection)

Two of the main sources of revenue-earning freight traffic in the Chesterfield area were the ironworks at Sheepbridge and at Staveley. 0–4–0ST DNT was supplied new to the Staveley Iron Company in 1949 having been built by W.G. Bagnall (works number 2907). A powerful looking engine, DNT had 16 in × 24 in cylinders, 3 ft 6 in diameter wheels and an angular saddle tank, which was unusual on Bagnalls. The photograph was taken in 1965 shortly before DNT was withdrawn. (Vic Hall)

Returning to the Midland's Chesterfield–Derby line we come to Wingfield, situated between Ambergate and Stretton. Described as 'the most perfect of all station houses', Wingfield was a Francis Thompson masterpiece designed in the Georgian style with paired ornamental chimneys. The station closed to goods traffic on 2 December 1963 and to passengers on 2 January 1967. (Author's Collection)

Numbered DY272 in the Derby Glass Plate Register, this intriguing picture is in fact the first one of a locomotive to be listed, the previous 271 plates being various towns and tourist sites. Taken at Wingfield at some time in the late 1890s, though possibly earlier, it shows a Bury 0–4–0 lying abandoned in the station yard. (NRM/DY272)

THE ASHOVER LIGHT RAILWAY

THE ASHOVER LIGHT RAILWAY.

TIME TABLE. From JUNE 6th, 1936, until further notice.
ON WEDNESDAYS, SATURDAYS and SUNDAYS ONLY.

UP TRAINS.	WEDNESDAYS & SATURDAYS ONLY.						SUNDAY			DOWN TRAINS.	WEDNESDAYS & SATURDAYS ONLY.						SUNDAY		
	a.m.	a.m.	a.m.	p.m.	p.m.	p.m.	p.m.	p.m.	p.m.		a.m.	a.m.	p.m.	p.m.	p.m.	p.m.	p.m.	p.m.	p.m.
CLAY CROSS and EGSTOW dep.										Ashover (Butts) dep.									
CHESTERFIELD ROAD "										Salter Lane (H) "									
Holmgate (H) "										FALLGATE "									
Springfield (H) "										Milltown (H) "									
Clay Lane (H) "										Dale Bank (H) "									
STRETTON "										Woolley "									
Hurst Lane (H) "										Hurst Lane (H) "									
Woolley "										STRETTON "									
Dale Bank (H) "										Clay Lane (H) "									
Milltown (H) "										Springfield (H) "									
FALLGATE "										Holmgate (H) "									
Salter Lane (H) "										CHESTERFIELD ROAD "									
Ashover (Butts) arr.										CLAY CROSS and EGSTOW arr.									

Note :— (H) denotes that the Trains will only stop at these Halts when required to set down passengers & pick up passengers by request.
Passengers joining trains at the Halts should be there five minutes before the time shown in time-table.

CHEAP RETURN TICKETS

CLAY CROSS, any station, and STRETTON, 9d. return.
" Single Journey Fares at Ordinary Rates. "

Jos. Spriggs & Sons, General Printers, Clay Cross.

G. H. WILBRAHAM, Manager.

The 2 ft gauge Ashover Light Railway was one of the last narrow gauge lines to be built in the UK, opening in April 1925 and running from Clay Cross & Egstow via Holmgate, Springfield, Clay Lane, Stretton, Hurst Lane, Woolley, Dalebank, Milltown, Fallgate, and Salter Lane to Ashover (Butts). The railway carried both passengers and freight alike including quarry traffic, the motive power originally consisting of four ex-WD 4–6–0PTs and Guy, Peggy, Hummy and Joan. The locomotives were all products of the Baldwin Locomotive Works in the United States and had been built for war service on the Western Front. Two further engines, Bridget and a second Guy were bought from T.W. Ward for £300 apiece in 1925. The original passenger service included seven trains each way on weekdays, eight each way on Saturdays and four on the Sabbath. Mixed trains were operated on weekdays but not during school holidays or at weekends when separate stone trains ran. Initial passenger returns were good (over 5,000 people were carried on the second week of operation), but competition soon reared its ugly head in the form of an improved bus service. From October 1931 the winter passenger service was abandoned, resuming for the 1932 Easter holiday period. For the next four years the ALR operated a summer season passenger service three days a week and special trains at Easter and Whitsun. Receipts continued to fall, and the decision to abandon passenger services 'until further notice' was taken in September 1936. Freight trains continued to run and some opencast traffic was generated during 1942 from a black shale seam at Woodthorpe Hall. In January 1950 Butts Quarry closed. The ALR lingered on just two months, closing on 31 March.

Bridget taking on water at Fallgate, 25 July 1935. She differed from the original four engines in that she was fitted with a full length cab throughout her career. Out of use by 1945, she was cannibalized to keep *Peggy* and *Joan* running. What remained of her was cut up at Clay Cross in May 1951. (LGRP)

Joan at the head of a mixed train at Ashover, 25 July 1935. This locomotive hauled the inaugural passenger train on 6 April 1925. In 1948 she was fitted with the left-hand tank off *Bridget*, complete with its nameplate, thereby running as *Joan* on the right side and *Bridget* on the left. She was cut up in May 1951. (LGRP)

AROUND THE EREWASH VALLEY

Westhouses & Blackwell, on the line between Chesterfield and Ilkeston, plays host to an Up passenger train. The original station was named West House or West Houses (it depended on where one looked) and closed in August 1865. The newer station pictured here closed to goods traffic on 2 November 1964 and completely on 2 January 1967. (M.L. Knighton Collection)

Pye Hill Colliery, 1967. An 1891 vintage Andrew Barclay 0–4–0ST (works number 705) simmers in the afternoon sunshine. In common with all Pye Hill engines, the cab and boiler fittings have been reduced to meet the restricted loading gauge. (Vic Hall)

Crosshill & Codnor on the Midland line from Ripley to Langley Mill opened in June 1890. This picturesque but somewhat under-used station closed in January 1917 under the war economy measures. Reopened in May 1920 following local appeals which didn't translate into paying customers, the station finally closed its doors on 4 May 1926. (M.L. Knighton Collection)

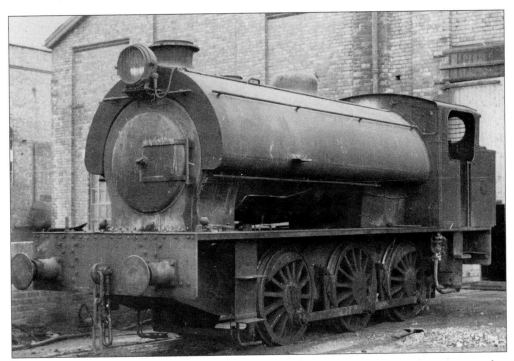

The Austerity 0–6–0ST was produced in large numbers by several manufacturers including Hunslet, Hudswell Clarke & Co. and Robert Stephenson & Hawthorns, and many examples have survived into preservation. The design originated with Hunslet's 18 in model, which, after modifications, was chosen by the Ministry of Supply as its standard shunting engine during the Second World War. Photographed at Coppice Colliery in 1964 is Hunslet 2882/1943. Supplied new to the WD as its WD75035, she was sold to the NCB East Midlands Division in 1947. (Vic Hall)

Ilkeston Town, terminus of a short branch from Ilkeston Junction, opened in 1847. Originally known as Ilkeston, it was closed to passengers by the Midland in May 1870, but reopened as Ilkeston Town on 1 July 1879. Passenger traffic was always light if not downright invisible; the GNR station, though further out of town, offered a faster service to Nottingham. The station succumbed to the inevitable on 16 June 1947. (M.L. Knighton Collection)

Stanton No. 3 was supplied new to Stanton Ironworks in 1909 by the Avonside Engine Company of Bristol (works number 1567). Rebuilt in 1920 and again in 1938, the old girl was still in use when this picture was taken in 1964. Points worth noting are the windows cut out of the back of the cab to give the crew a better view when shunting, the bell-shaped dome, tapered chimney and, unusual for an industrial locomotive, outside steampipes. (Vic Hall)

Shunting at Stanton Ironworks in 1964 was *Sheepbridge No. 28*, a powerful looking brute built by the Yorkshire Engine Company in 1943 (works number 2413). The engine was delivered new to Sheepbridge Ironworks near Chesterfield but later transferred to Stanton. It was a typical Yorkshire product with full-length saddle tank, squat boiler mountings and safety valves on the dome. Note also the operating wheel on the smokebox door instead of a handle and the sloping back to the cab. (Vic Hall)

One of Stanton's famous crane-tanks, *Stanton No. 33*, at work. Built by Andrew Barclay in 1937 (works number 2030) Stanton No. 33 was one of no fewer than nine such engines on the Stanton Ironworks roster. Crane-tanks were ideal workhorses, being able to perform both lifting and shunting operations. Their only drawback was that the crane jib itself couldn't be raised or lowered as this would have altered the centre of gravity of the engine. Therefore the crane was used for straight lift and slew round operations. (Vic Hall)

Stanton No. 36 was one of a pair of useful-looking 0–6–0STs supplied by Andrew Barclay in 1942. Note that the dome is forward of the saddle tank filler cap and that the safety valves are set in the tank. (Vic Hall)

The only side tank to be obtained by Stanton Ironworks was *Stanton No. 38*, built by Andrew Barclay in 1949 (works number 2273). The side tanks slope forward in order to improve visibility for the crew when shunting. This engine was the last new steam locomotive to be purchased by them. (Vic Hall)

In 1927 Beyer Peacock & Company supplied three 2–6–0+0–6–2 Garretts to the LMS. Designed to haul heavy coal trains between Toton and Brent, these powerful superheated engines had 18½in × 26 in cylinders, 5 ft 3 in driving wheels and a boiler pressure of 190 psi, giving a tractive effort of 45,620 lb. In 1930 a further thirty Garretts were delivered incorporating a number of design modifications, including increased coal capacity, strengthened frames and taller chimneys and domes. Unfortunately, these excellent machines suffered a number of defects as the LMS insisted on influencing the design instead of letting the experts at Peacocks get on with it. The LMS suggested short travel valves and small axlebox bearings, while Beyer Peacock experience called for large bearings and long travel valves. In the late 1930s a proposal to rebuild the Garretts with new frames, axles and axleboxes was shelved because of the cost. Withdrawals began in 1955, the last Garrett surviving until 1958. The picture shows Garrett No. 4972 as delivered to the LMS fitted with an ordinary coal bunker, a notorious device prone to filling the cab with dust when running bunker first. (D.J. Gibson Collection)

Garrett No. 47993 at Toton, 9 October 1954. (C.M. & J.M. Bentley)

Garrett No. 47976 trundles into Toton, 9 October 1954. The front-end tender held 3,030 gallons, the rear 1,470 gallons, while the capacity of the rotating bunker was 9 tons. In 1931 a series of trials were held to assess a number of design modifications carried out on the second batch of locomotives. It was found that coal consumption was reduced by 12 per cent and water by 5 per cent when hauling a 1,200 ton train. The best steaming results were obtained when burning coal from Grimethorpe Colliery. (C.M. & J.M. Bentley)

On 26 September 1847 the Midland Railway opened its Erewash Valley line from Trent Junction northwards to connect with the Derby–Leeds line at Clay Cross. Some of the intermediate stations were Sandiacre (later Stapleford & Sandiacre), Stanton (later Stanton Gate), Ilkeston Junction, Shipley (later Shipley Gate), Heanor Junction and Langley Mill. By 1854 there was a spur connecting with Stanton Ironworks, the Erewash line itself rapidly developing into a main line to the north. The sheer volume of mineral and passenger traffic soon required the tracks to be quadrupled. The picture shows Stanton Gate in 1952. The quadruple tracks can be seen clearly; the spur to the left is the line to Mapperley. (D.J. Gibson Collection)

ALONG THE
RIPLEY BRANCH

The Little Eaton Gangway opened in May 1795 to carry coal and other freight from Smithy Houses to a
nearby branch of the Derby Canal. The picture, taken in about 1908, shows a gang on the Little
Eaton–Wharf section. The gang consisted of four horses harnessed in single file hauling eight wagons. The
carter walked at the head of the ensemble, positioned by the leading horse. The harnessing was designed to
allow any horse to be changed without having to interfere with the harnessing of the others.
(Author's Collection)

An interesting array of pointwork on the approach to Little Eaton Wharf. The points were worked simply enough by kicking or levering over a moving tongue pivoted at the head into the direction required. One of the advantages of this type of trackwork was that wagons would still run even if the rails were out of gauge by an inch or two. In the background can be seen a wagon chassis (tram) without its body (box). On the wharf a horse appears to be hard at work doing a spot of shunting. Also in the picture is the Midland Railway goods shed. (Author's Collection)

The wagons used on the Gangway consisted of a chassis (tram) and a body (box). There were at least three types of body in use: the main type held around 48 cwt of coal, the second type had slatted sides and was used for carrying stone, while the third was for general freight. The boxes were designed to be lifted off the trams by crane and loaded directly into a waiting narrowboat for onward shipment to Derby. This was in effect an early form of containerization. In this picture a loaded box is about to be lowered into the narrowboat. The Midland Railway signalbox is in the background. (Author's Collection)

Loading is underway at the wharf. In the background a box has been lifted clear of its tram. The horse might be the local shunter as older horses were kept at the wharf to perform this duty, their principal task being to assist in the making up of gangs of empties. The inverted fish belly pattern rails can be seen, these being similar to those laid in the eighteenth century. The house served as the agent's office. (Author's Collection)

A Nottingham district set at Little Eaton, 31 December 1915. On the buffer beam is the inscription 'Nottingham district – 9 ft 3 in wide'. Also note that the guards door opens inwards. (M.L. Knighton Collection)

Originally called Smithy Houses, Denby lost its passenger service on 1 June 1930 and its goods facilities on 4 January 1965. Denby is now the northern terminus of the Ripley branch, the sole reason for the line's continued existence being to serve Denby Disposal Point. However, reduced output since 1993 led to fewer trains being run to Drakelow C power station. (M.L. Knighton Collection)

The prototype Sentinel lightweight steam railcar on trials with the LMS is seen here at Ripley on 12 March 1925. The brute was purchased by the LMS, who ordered another twelve units, each capable of carrying forty-four passengers. (NRM/DY13615)

In the 1890s the Ripley branch was extended to Butterley. This postcard from before the First World War shows a train bound for either Ambergate or Ripley. Closed to passengers on 16 June 1947 and to goods traffic on 2 November 1964, the site was later occupied by the Midland Railway Project Group and is now the headquarters of the Midland Railway Centre. The centre boasts a 57 acre museum site, a 3½ mile standard gauge line complete with restored signals and signalboxes, a new Butterley station (formerly Whitwell station building) and the redeveloped Swanwick Junction station. There is also a narrow gauge line which is to be extended through a 35 acre country park. The centre is home to an exciting collection of locomotives and rolling stock. For details of events contact 01773 747674 or 01773 570140. (Author's Collection)

Butterley station on the Midland Railway Centre's standard gauge line. The signalbox at the end of the platform is in fact just stored there for possible future use elsewhere on the line. (Author's Collection)

Class 08 No. 08590 at Butterley, May 1997. (Author's Collection)

THE WIRKSWORTH BRANCH

0–4–4T No. 58077 standing in the branch platform at Duffield at the head of an SLS / MLS railtour. The engine carries a 17B (Burton) shedplate and was one of the class to be rebuilt with a Belpaire boiler.
(C.M. & J.M. Bentley)

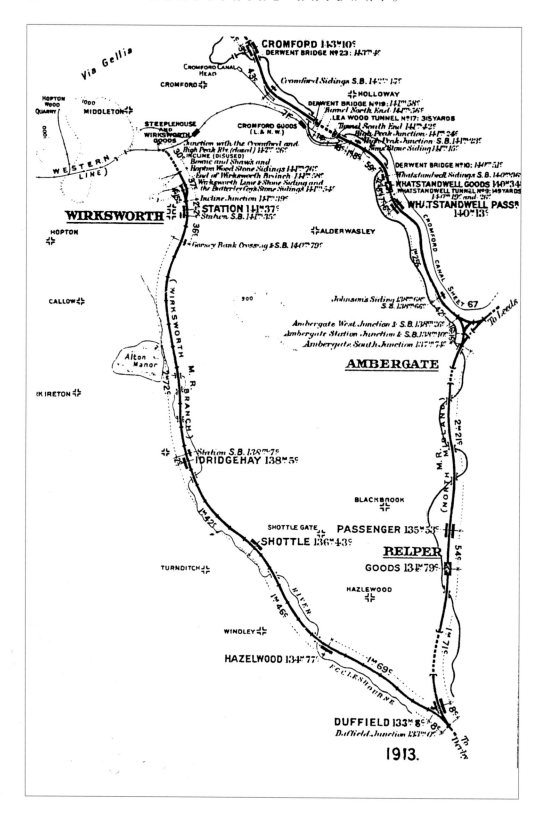

WESTERN LINE

Via Gellis

HOPTON WOOD QUARRY

MIDDLETON

STEEPLEHOUSE AND WIRKSWORTH GOODS

CROMFORD 143ᴹ10ᶜ
DERWENT BRIDGE Nº 23: 147ᴹ4ᶜ

CROMFORD CANAL HEAD

CROMFORD

CROMFORD GOODS

Cromford Sidings S.B. 142ᴹ17ᶜ

HOLLOWAY

DERWENT BRIDGE Nº19: 141ᴹ54ᶜ
Tunnel North End. 141ᴹ56ᶜ
LEA WOOD TUNNEL Nº17: 315 YARDS
Tunnel South End 141ᴹ42ᶜ
High Peak Junction 141ᴹ24ᶜ
High Peak Junction S.B. 141ᴹ23ᶜ
Sims Stone Siding 141ᴹ16ᶜ

Junction with the Cromford and
High Peak Rly. (closed) 142ᴹ36ᶜ
INCLINE (DISUSED)
Bonsic and Shaws and
Hopton Wood Stone Sidings 141ᴹ76ᶜ
End of Wirksworth Branch. 141ᴹ58ᶜ
Wirksworth Lane & Stone Siding and
the Butterley Cork Stone Sidings 141ᴹ54ᶜ

Incline Junction 141ᴹ49ᶜ

WIRKSWORTH

STATION 141ᴹ37ᶜ
Station S.B. 141ᴹ35ᶜ

HOPTON

DERWENT BRIDGE Nº10: 141ᴹ51ᶜ
Whatstandwell Sidings S.B. 140ᴹ36ᶜ
WHATSTANDWELL GOODS 140ᴹ34ᶜ
WHATSTANDWELL TUNNEL Nº9: 149 YARDS
140ᴹ19ᶜ and. 26ᶜ
WHATSTANDWELL PASSʳ
140ᴹ13ᶜ

ALDERWASLEY

Garsey Bank Crossing & S.B. 140ᴹ79ᶜ

CALLOW

Johnson's Siding 139ᴹ68ᶜ
S.B. 139ᴹ66ᶜ

SHEET 67

To Leeds

Ambergate West Junction & S.B. 138ᴹ26ᶜ
Ambergate Station Junction & S.B. 138ᴹ10ᶜ
Ambergate South Junction 137ᴹ74ᶜ

Alton Manor

(WIRKSWORTH M.R. BRANCH)

IRELTON

AMBERGATE

Station S.B. 138ᴹ7ᶜ
IDRIDGEHAY 138ᴹ5ᶜ

BLACKBROOK

TURNDITCH

SHOTTLE GATE
SHOTTLE 136ᴹ43ᶜ

PASSENGER 135ᴹ53ᶜ

RELPER

GOODS 134ᴹ79ᶜ

HAZLEWOOD

WINDLEY

HAZELWOOD 134ᴹ77ᶜ

RIVER ECCLESBOURNE

DUFFIELD 133ᴹ8ᶜ
Duffield Junction 133ᴹ0ᶜ

To Derby

1913.

The SLS/MLS railtour of the Wirksworth branch rolls into Idridgehay, 25 April 1953. The station was designed by J.S. Crossley and consisted of two pavilions linked by the booking hall to give an H-shaped building. The prototype for this design was Pinxton & Selston, but Idridgehay, Shottle and Hazelwood was the first Crossley type to be completed, the pattern being repeated throughout the Midland. (C.M. & J.M. Bentley)

The level crossing at Idridgehay, *c.* 1900. The level crossing gates were removed in the early 1980s, and the road traffic lights are powered by solar panels. (Author's Collection)

M&GNR 4–4–0T No. 10 at Wirksworth with an auto-train, 1906. The Midland had four auto-trains, each comprising a M&GNR 4–4–0T and a former Pullman parlour car. Services operated included Harpenden–Hemel Hempstead, Derby–Melbourne, Derby–Ripley and Derby–Wirksworth. These trains operated from 1906 to 1912, when the tank engines were returned to the M&GNR. (Author's Collection)

An excellent view of Wirksworth yard, 25 April 1953. In the distance are the goods shed and the two-road engine shed (that's the one with the wagon sticking out of it), behind which was a 42 ft turntable and a water tower. The line to the right of the engine shed connects with Bowne & Shaw's quarry. (C.M. & J.M. Bentley)

Holwell No. 3 was built by the Tyneside firm of Black Hawthorn in 1873 (works number 266) and arrived at Bowne & Shaw, Wirksworth, from Harlaxton Ironstone Mines in November 1946. The engine's original owner was the contractor Walter Scott, in whose service she carried the name *Wellington*. Acquired by the Holwell Iron Company, she was rebuilt in 1894, 1901, 1911 and 1935, the modifications including a new chimney, mechanical lubricator and cast-iron brake blocks. The extension to the right-hand side of the cab was a Wirksworth addition. Even in 1970, when this picture was taken, *Holwell No. 3*'s Black Hawthorn pedigree was still evident: short flat-sided saddle tank, curved weather board, handbrake working on the rear wheels only and spring balance safety valves mounted over the firebox. *Holwell No. 3* remained in regular service until 1966 when the quarry bought a Baguley 0–4–0 diesel from Ind Coope. At the end of 1977 *Holwell No. 3* was sold for preservation and is now on the Tanfield Railway. (Vic Hall)

No. 58077 approaches Duffield. (C.M. & J.M. Bentley)

MIDLAND RAILWAY
RAIL MOTOR SERVICE
TO AND FROM DERBY.

Commencing March 1st, 1906,

THE FOLLOWING RAIL MOTOR SERVICES WILL BE IN OPERATION ON WEEKDAYS, IN ADDITION TO THE EXISTING ORDINARY SERVICE:—

DERBY & MELBOURNE.

		a.m.	p.m.	p.m.			a.m.	p.m.	p.m.
DERBY	dep.	7 40	12 5	4 55	MELBOURNE	dep.	8 12	12 38	5 23
Chellaston	,,	7 49	12 15	5 4	Chellaston	,,	8 21	12 47	5 32
MELBOURNE	arr.	7 56	12 22	5 11	DERBY	arr.	8 32	12 56	5 40

DERBY & WIRKSWORTH.

		a.m.	p.m.				a.m.	p.m.	
DERBY	dep.	8 45	1 55	...	WIRKSWORTH	dep.	9 45	2 50	...
Nottingham Road	,,	8 52	1 59	...	Idridgehay	,,	9 53	2 58	...
Duffield	arr.	9 1	2 8	...	Shottle	,,	9 58	3 3	...
	dep.	9 8	2 12	...	Hazelwood	,,	10 3	3 8	...
Hazelwood	,,	9 11	2 17	...	Duffield	arr.	10 7	3 12	...
Shottle	,,	9 16	2 22	...		dep.	10 9	3 15	...
Idridgehay	,,	9 21	2 27	...	DERBY	arr.	10 18	3 25	...
WIRKSWORTH	arr.	9 29	2 35	...					

DERBY & RIPLEY.

		a.m.					a.m.		
DERBY	dep.	10 32	...	...	RIPLEY	dep.	11 25	...	...
Little Eaton	,,	10 41	...	...	Denby	,,	11 32	...	...
Coxbench	,,	10 47	...	...	Kilburn	,,	11 36	...	...
Kilburn	,,	10 53	...	...	Coxbench	,,	11 42	...	...
Denby	,,	10 58	...	...	Little Eaton	,,	11 48	...	...
RIPLEY	arr.	11 6	...	...	DERBY	arr.	11 57	...	...

THIRD CLASS ORDINARY FARES ONLY WILL BE CHARGED.
Tickets may be obtained at the Booking Offices in the usual way.

Derby, Feb. 1906.   JOHN MATHIESON, General Manager.

Bemrose & Sons Limited, Printers to the Company.

Having run round the main line, No. 58077 awaits a road north. (C.M. & J.M. Bentley)

LNWR & NSR LINES

A major headache for the C&HPR was that of securing adequate water supplies for stationary engines, locomotives and cottages along the route. The problem was solved by converting a number of obsolete LNWR locomotive tenders into mobile water tanks. Some were four-wheelers dating from the 1850s. Others were six-wheelers with the middle set removed so that they could be taken up and down the inclines. The tanks were usually filled at Cromford Goods, the supply being from a nearby natural spring, though it is known that water was also obtained from the Buxton end of the line. About a hundred tanks of water were sent from Cromford every month to various sites along the line including Sheep Pasture Top, Middleton Top, Longcliffe, Parsley Hay, Alsop-en-le-Dale and Hurdlow. Even in the BR era twenty-one old tenders were retained, some over a hundred years old. The picture, taken in 1931, is looking in the direction of Cromford Goods Wharf. The tanks are at the bottom of the Cromford Incline, the furthest away from the camera being an old four-wheeler. (LGRP)

Steeplehouse, March 1932. The track turning sharp left is the spur into the goods yard. The large building served for many years as the stables for railway cart horses; the yard office is in fact the small structure to the left of the picture. The line at middle left is the main line to Parsley Hay and the one where the wagons are stabled served Middlepeak Quarry. The line on the right-hand side leads to Killer's Middleton Quarry. (LGRP)

In 1931 the LMS began transferring ex-North London Railway 0–6–0Ts to the C&HPR. These sturdy engines had a tractive effort of 18,140 lb, their short wheelbase making them ideal for the sharp curves at locations like Steeplehouse. A total of ten ex-NLR tanks worked the line at various times. One of them, No. 27521, was involved in a fatal accident on 6 October 1937, when it became derailed at the bottom of Hopton incline and rolled 25 ft down the embankment. The locomotive came to a rest in the roadway surrounded by the debris from several wagons; the driver unfortunately did not survive. The engine lay blocking the road for a couple of weeks before it was dismantled and taken to Derby Works, where it was examined prior to being scrapped. The picture shows No. 58850 (ex-LMS No. 27505) at Middleton Top. This engine holds the distinction of being the last of its type to work on the C&HPR, where it shunted away until early in 1960. Withdrawn in September of that year, No. 58850 was later acquired by the Bluebell Railway. (LGRP)

CROMFORD AND HIGH PEAK
RAILWAY.

TIME TABLE for APRIL, 1874, and until further Notice.

DOWN — STATIONS

High Peak June.
Cromford
Steep Turnpike
Steeplehouse
Middleton
Hopton
Hockley's Siding
Longcliffe
Bloore's Siding
Minninglow
Friden
Parsley Hay
Hurdlow
Hindlow
Harpur Hill
Bunsall
Ladmanlow
Shallcross
Whaley Bridge

UP — STATIONS

Whaley Bridge
Shallcross
Bunsall
Ladmanlow
Harpur Hill
Hindlow
Hurdlow
Parsley Hay
Friden
Minninglow
Bloore's Siding
Longcliffe
Buckley's Siding
Hopton
Middleton
Steeplehouse
Steep Pasture
Cromford
High Peak June.

REGULATIONS FOR WORKING BETWEEN LADMANLOW AND HARPUR HILL.

The Line between Ladmanlow and Harpur Hill must be worked by an Engine Staff lettered L. & HH. All Engines passing between these points must carry the Staff, with the Exception of the 8.0 a.m. and 10.55 a.m. Trains from Ladmanlow, and the 10.15 a.m. and 3.15 p.m. Trains from Harpur Hill. The Enginemen in charge of these four Trains must see the Staff at the Starting points immediately before proceeding on their journey.

At Ladmanlow between the Buxton Lime Co.'s Branch and the Coal Siding, the Line must be worked by Signals from Ladmanlow; and Engines must not pass over this length at a greater Speed than Four Miles per Hour. The Arm on that side of the Signal Post which is nearest to the Main Line of Rails, is the Signal for Engines from Whaley Bridge to Cromford, or Cromford to Whaley Bridge. The Arm on the side of the Signal Post, away from the Main Line, is the Signal for Engines between Ladmanlow and the Coal Branch. An Engineman from the Main Line must give One Whistle, and from the Branch or Coal Siding Two Whistles, and must not proceed beyond the Signal until it is lowered.

A paper ticket for the Ladmanlow branch authorizing the driver to proceed through the section. The driver was shown the staff then issued with the ticket. This procedure allowed consecutive moves in the same direction without the need to install an electric token machine. (Author's Collection)

In 1862 the LNWR were concerned that the small workshops at Cromford would soon become inadequate for the task of maintaining the line's locomotives and the mobile water tanks. Ladmanlow was recommended as an alternative site. It was within easy reach of both Crewe and Longsight and it was also situated on the longest stretch of level ground on the entire C&HPR. However, the move never materialized and Ladmanlow was allowed to drift into relative obscurity once the Shallcross Yard–Bunsall section was abandoned in 1892. The picture shows the yard from the level crossing over the Buxton–Leek road and is looking towards the abandoned section which then lay several hundred yards round the corner. (LGRP)

Looking the other way. The signal controls access to the Grinn Quarry branch. (LGRP)

An enthusiasts' special trundles into Ladmanlow behind 0–6–0 3F No. 43618 on 23 April 1963. These two pictures show just how near Ladmanlow yard was to the town. Another interesting fact is that the level crossing was situated on a blind corner for road traffic coming out of Buxton. (C.M. & J.M. Bentley)

Parsley Hay was the junction of the LNWR's Ashbourne branch and the C&HPR. The view, taken in 1932, is of the north end of the station looking towards Buxton. The goods yard is on the right, the junction with the C&HPR being at the southern end. In keeping with a number of installations on this line, much of Parsley Hay was constructed out of timber. (LGRP)

Hartington on the line to Ashbourne, photographed just eighteen months before closure to passenger traffic. Goods traffic continued until 6 July 1964, with demolition taking place a few months later. The signalbox remains *in situ* and is preserved intact including the frame. The trackbed now forms the Tissington Trail, which is open all year round. Car parking is available at Hartington in the former goods yard behind the signalbox. The view is looking towards Parsley Hay. (LGRP)

Overgrown and almost forgotten: Ashbourne Tunnel about fifteen years after rail services had ended. The site of the former LNWR/NSR joint station is behind the photographer. Passenger services ended on 1 November 1954, though goods traffic continued until June 1964. For a few months Ashbourne lingered on as a non-rail-connected depot, final closure coming in February 1965. (Tony Griffin)

NSR 0–6–2T at Ashbourne, 1916. The original NSR station closed to passengers on 4 August 1899 having been replaced by a new LNWR/NSR joint station. The NSR goods depot survived to be incorporated into the joint property. (LGRP)

Photographed at John Knowles Ltd, Woodville, in 1966 is Hunslet 0–4–0ST John Knowles No. 4 built in 1920 (works number 1403). The flat-sided saddle tank covers only the boiler barrel, the dome is placed centrally and the engine is also fitted with Ross pop safety valves. (Vic Hall)

AROUND & ABOUT

In November 1939 the military took over the Derby–Ashby line from Chellaston East Junction to a point 1 mile north of Ashby-de-la-Zouch as No. 2 Railway Training Centre. A large marshalling yard was constructed at King's Newton, the centre being involved in all types of training for both British and United States troops. Among the US units to visit were the 761 Railway Transportation Company, 755 Railway Shops Battalion and the 763 Railway Shops Battalion. On a visit to Melbourne in October 1943 R.C. Riley noted the following locomotives: WD99 (ex-GWR 2528), half a dozen ex-MR 1F 0–6–0Ts including Nos 1666, 1708, 1751, 1788, 1839 and 1890. There was also a batch of USTC 0–6–0Ts comprising Nos WD1255, 1387, 1407, 1410, 1939, 1944, 1968, 1970 and 1971. Also knocking about were an ex-LNWR 0-6-0ST, a WD 0-6-0ST No. WD5061 and a 0-6-0D No. 4564. The picture dates from 1942 and shows engineers at work in King's Newton sidings. (Author's Collection)

Castle Donington & Shardlow is just over the border in Leicestershire but is typical of a number of small stations. The line between Trent Junction and Weston-on-Trent opened in 1869, being extended in 1873 to the Midland main line at Stenson by way of Chellaston East and Chellaston West Junctions. The line offered a better route to the south-west and Birmingham for Erewash Valley mineral traffic. This station lost its passenger trains on 22 September 1930 and closed completely on 1 May 1967. (Author's Collection)

The MCR opened its line from Derby to Nottingham on 30 May 1839, the intermediate stations being Burrowash, Breaston, Long Eaton and Beeston. When scheduled services commenced there were five trains each way on weekdays and two on Sundays. Before the end of the year Draycote too had opened for business. Later renamed Draycott, the station closed to passengers on 14 February 1966 having lost its goods traffic seven months earlier. Note the dip in the platform to allow barrows to be wheeled across the tracks. (Author's Collection)

An extract from the Luftwaffe's *Objektbilder* for the north Midlands. This booklet of heavily retouched photographs was issued to aircrews as an aid to locating targets. The picture itself was taken in 1935. The cameraman has his back to Spondon station and is looking in the direction of Chaddesden Sidings. The line veering off to the left leads to Derby. Note that the dual carriageway over the railway is incomplete. (Author's Collection)

Doing its bit for the war effort is LMS No. 20002, built in 1866 and the last surviving member of Kirtley's 156 Class of 2–4–0 passenger engines. A total of twenty-nine were built including five by Kirtley's successor Samuel Johnson. All were rebuilt by Johnson with 18 in × 24 in cylinders, new boilers and an increased heating surface. In 1907 Richard Deeley renumbered the survivors Nos 1–22 inclusive and all of them passed into LMS ownership. When the LMS withdrew No. 1, they repainted her in Midland colours and gave her her old duplicate number of No. 156A. She was then stored at Derby along with a Kirtley goods engine (No. 421), an ex-North London 4–4–0T and a Johnson 0–4–4T. But any thoughts of preserving these wonderful old engines were dashed in 1932 with the arrival of William Stanier from Swindon. For some reason now lost (or was it Stanier acting the new kid on the block?) he ordered them to be scrapped. Meanwhile old No. 2 somehow managed to linger on, though she had been renumbered No. 20002. In 1948, after eighty-two years of service, she emerged from Derby Works carrying her old duplicate number No. 158A. Now a part of the national collection, No. 158A is at the Midland Railway Centre, Butterley. (Imperial War Museum)

Spinner No. 600 prior to her being fitted with Deeley vacuum control gear for working the Superintendent's saloon. Based at Derby, No. 600 worked until September 1928 when she was withdrawn. (Author's Collection)

Shunting at British Celanese Works, Spondon, in 1965 is Hawthorn Leslie 0–4–0ST *Henry*, built in 1901 (works number 2491). One of three saddle tanks working here in the 1960s, the other two were *George* and *Victory*. (Vic Hall)

Markeaton Park's latest attraction, the 15 in gauge coal-fired steam locomotive *Markeaton Lady* makes her first official trip on the half mile long Markeaton Park Light Railway, 24 October 1966. Built by the Exmoor Railway of Bratton Fleming, Devon, at a cost of £40,000, the steam engine brings character to the line whose only other form of motive power is a four-wheel petrol locomotive named *Cromwell*. The MPLR was the brainchild of Mr L. Searle, who built the first section in the mid-1980s. Circumstances prevented Mr Searle from completing the project and ownership was transferred to the father and son team of John E. and John A. Bull. This led to the line being extended and purpose-built air-braked rolling stock being acquired. HM Inspectorate approval was granted on 24 September 1996. (Courtesy Tony Griffin)

The RAF provides the gate guard at Friargate station goods depot, 11 October 1939. In the background is the large warehouse built by the GNR, which could be used as a bonded store as well as for general goods. (*Derby Evening Telegraph*)

The LNER's concrete sleeper plant at Friargate employed female labour throughout the war years. This picture was taken in December 1942. (Author's Collection)

GREAT NORTHERN

Mickleover & Radbourne on the GNR looking towards Etwall. This station was 2½ miles west of Derby Friargate and lost its daily passenger service on 4 December 1939, along with Egginton Junction and Etwall, following the withdrawal of LNER services to Burton-upon-Trent. Excursion trains continued to call here for a number of years but total closure came on 3 February 1964. (Author's Collection)

L1 tank No. 67756 at Friargate. One hundred of these two-cylinder engines were built between 1946 and 1950, and all had comparatively short careers before being displaced by DMUs or other steam locomotives. The L1s were the mainstay of Friargate's Nottingham service in the late 1950s, but the entire class had been withdrawn by the end of 1962 and were superseded by Ivatt 2–6–0s, which remained until the line closed. One of the advantages Derby Friargate station had over the Midland station was its proximity to the town centre. There were four platforms for passengers, a three-storey goods warehouse and spacious goods yard with a cattle station. The GNR also built a four-road engine shed and servicing facility including a turntable. The Friargate line benefited both the GNR and NSR. Passenger and freight traffic gradually increased and in 1896 the companies reached an accord on reciprocal running powers. The agreement allowed for the NSR to work between Alsager and Colwick, and the GNR was permitted to work through goods trains from Colwick to Alsager and between Peterborough and Stoke-on-Trent. This close-working relationship was later extended to allow the through working of passenger coaches on summer trains to holiday resorts. (Chris Canner)

TRAIN SERVICE 15th JUNE to 6th SEPTEMBER 1964

OR UNTIL FURTHER NOTICE

(subject to alteration)

WEEKDAYS

		am	am	am	SO am	am	A SO am	am	SO am	SO am	B SO am	C SX am	SO am	SX am	D SO am	SO am	SX am	SO am	am	SO am	SO am	am	am	am	am	pm	pm			
DERBY Friargate ...dep.		...	5 35	...	6 20	7 10	...	...	...	8 10	8 20	8 20	...	8 55	9 30	...	...	9 50	1035	...	1155	...	1 0	...	...			
WEST HALLAM ... ,,		...	...	...	...	7 22	...	...	...	8 23	8 32	8 32	...	9 8	9 42	...	...	10 3	1047	...	12 7	...	1 12	...	...			
ILKESTON North ... ,,		...	5 52	...	6 37	7 28	...	...	...	8 30	8 38	8 38	...	9 15	9 48	...	...	1010	1053	...	1213	...	1 18	...	...			
AWSWORTH ... ,,		...	...	...	6 42	7 32	...	...	...	8 35	8 42	8 42	...	9 20	9 52	...	...	1015	1057	...	1217	...	1 22	...	...			
KIMBERLEY East ... ,,		...	6 0	...	6 48	7 37	...	...	...	8 41	8 47	8 47	...	9 26	9 57	...	...	1021	11 2	...	1222	...	1 27	...	...			
BASFORD North ... ,,		...	6 7	...	6 56	7 44	...	...	...	8 49	8 54	8 54	...	9 34	10 4	...	...	1029	11 9	...	1229	...	1 34	...	...			
NEW BASFORD ... ,,		...	6 12	...	7 49		...	...	...				...			...	...	1035	...	...	1234	...	1 39	...	...			
NOTTINGHAM {Victoria arr.		...	6 16	...	7 47	7 54	...	...	...	8 57	9 2	9 2	...	9 42	1012	...	...	1039	1117	...	1238	...	1 43	...	...			
{Victoria dep.		5 25	...	6 55	7 10	...	8	5	8 30	8 35	9 5	...	9 10	9 15	9 20	9 47	...	10 0	1020	1030	1045	...	1145	...	1255	...	...	
{London Road ...dep.																												
{High Level																												
NETHERFIELD & COLWICK ... ,,		5 33	...	6 58	7	7 20	8	9	8 33	8 39	...	...	9 18	...	...	...	...	1023	...	...	1148	...	1258	...	...			
RADCLIFFE-ON-TRENT ... ,,		5 40	...	7	7	...	8 17	8 38	8 47	9 15	...	9 20	9 23	9 30	...	...	...	1028	...	...	1153	...	1 3	...	...			
BINGHAM ... ,,		5 48	...	7 7	...	8 23	8 42	8 53	...	...	9 25	9 27	9 35	...	...	...	1032	...	...	1157	...	1 7	...	...			
ASLOCKTON ... ,,		5 52	...	7 13	...	8 31	8 48	9 1	...	...	9 33	9 33	9 43	...	...	...	1038	...	...	12 3	...	1 13	...	...			
ELTON & ORSTON ... ,,		...	...	7 17	...	...	8 52	...	...	...	9 37	...	...	...	...	...	1042	...	...	...	...	1 17	...	...			
BOTTESFORD ... ,,		...	...	7 21	...	...	8 56	...	...	...	9 41	...	...	...	...	...	1046	...	...	...	...	1 21	...	...			
		6 0	...	7 26	7 41	...	9 1	...	...	...	9 45	9 46	9 55	...	...	1027	1051	11 0	...	...	...	1 26	...	...			
GRANTHAM ... — arr.		6 14	...	7 40	...	...	9 15	...	...	...	10 0	...	...	...	...	11 5	...	...	...	1225	...	1 40	...	...			

A—Commences 4th July.
B—Runs until 3rd July.
C—Commences 6th July.
D—Runs 20th July to 14th August.

SO—Saturdays only.
SX—Saturdays excepted.
E—Runs 18th July 22nd August.

TRAIN SERVICE 15th JUNE to 6th SEPTEMBER 1964

OR UNTIL FURTHER NOTICE

(subject to alteration)

WEEKDAYS

														A SO			SO	SO	SO	SO	SO	SX	SX	SO	SO	SX	SO
	am	am	am	am	am	am	am	am	am	am	pm	am	pm	pm	pm	pm	pm	pm	pm	pm	pm	pm	pm	pm	pm	pm	pm
GRANTHAM ... ...dep.	...	6 0	6 35	...	7 24	...	7 50	...	9 25	1030	...	1130	...	...	1255	...	...	2 20	...	...	3 20	3 25	...	...	...	4 15	4 22
BOTTESFORD ... ... „	...	6 10	6 47	...	7 34	...	8 0	...	9 35	1040	...	1140	...	...	1 5	...	...	2 30	...	3 10	3 30	3 35	...	...	4 11	4 25	4 32
ELTON & ORSTON ... ... „	...	...	6 51	...	7 39	...	8 5	...	9 40	1045	...	1145	...	...	1 10	...	...	2 35	...	...	3 35	3 40	...	...	...	4 30	4 37
ASLOCKTON ... ... „	...	6 17	6 56	...	7 42	...	8 8	...	9 43	1048	...	1148	...	...	1 13	...	...	2 38	...	...	3 38	3 43	...	...	...	4 33	4 40
BINGHAM ... ... „	...	6 21	7 2	...	7 46	...	8 12	...	9 47	1052	...	1152	...	1257	1 17	...	...	2 42	2 56	...	3 43	3 47	...	...	...	4 37	4 44
RADCLIFFE-ON-TRENT ... ... „	...	6 27	7 9	...	7 52	...	8 18	...	9 53	1058	...	1158	...	1 5	1 23	...	...	2 48	3 4	...	3 48	3 53	...	...	...	4 43	4 50
NETHERFIELD & COLWICK ... „	...	6 34	7 17	...	8 0	...	8 26	...	10 1	11 6	...	12 6	...	1 15	1 31	...	...	2 56	3 14	...	3 56	4 1	...	...	...	4 51	4 58
NOTTINGHAM London Road High Level ... „	...	6 40	7 23	...	8 7	...	8 32	...	10 7	1112	...	1212	...	1 23	13 7	...	...	3 2	3 22	...	4 2	4 7	...	...	...	4 57	5 4
NOTTINGHAM Victoria ... arr.	...	6 43	7 26	...	8 10	...	8 35	...	1010	1115	...	1215	...	1 26	1 40	...	2 51	3 5	3 25	3 41	4 5	4 10	...	...	4 39	5 0	5 7
NOTTINGHAM Victoria ...dep.	6 15	...	...	7 35	...	8 20	...	9 30	...	...	12 5	...	1255	...	...	2 5	2 57	...	3 30	...	...	...	4 15	4 35	...	...	...
NEW BASFORD ... ... „	...	...	...	7 40	...	...	...	...	...	...	...	...	1 0	...	...	2 10	3 2	...	3 35	...	...	...	4 20	4 40	...	...	...
BASFORD North ... ... „	6 23	...	...	7 45	...	8 28	...	9 38	...	...	1213	...	1 5	...	...	2 15	3 8	...	3 41	...	...	...	4 25	4 46	...	...	...
KIMBERLEY East ... ... „	6 30	...	...	7 52	...	8 36	...	9 45	...	...	1220	...	1 12	...	...	2 22	3 16	...	3 49	...	...	...	4 32	4 54	...	...	...
AWSWORTH ... ... „	6 34	...	...	7 56	...	8 40	...	9 49	...	...	1224	...	1 16	...	...	2 26	3 21	...	3 54	...	...	...	4 36	4 59	...	...	...
ILKESTON North ... ... „	6 39	...	...	8 0	...	8 44	...	9 53	...	...	1228	...	1 20	...	...	2 30	3 26	...	3 59	...	...	...	4 40	5 4	...	...	...
WEST HALLAM ... ... „	6 44	...	...	8 5	...	8 49	...	9 58	...	...	1233	...	1 25	...	...	2 35	3 32	...	4 5	...	...	...	4 45	5 10	...	...	...
DERBY Friargate ... ... arr.	6 55	...	...	8 16	...	9 0	...	10 9	...	...	1244	...	1 36	...	...	2 46	3 43	...	4 16	...	...	...	4 56	5 21	...	...	...

A—Commences 4th July.
p—pm.

SX—Saturdays excepted.
SO—Saturdays only.

The GNR bridge over the River Derwent, 22 February 1979. By this time the bridge was painted pale green, the cantilevered footbridge had been removed and the former rail deck converted for pedestrian use. (Tony Griffin)

The end of the GNR viaduct at Breadsall was captured on film by Tony Griffin.

Ilkeston on the former GNR line from Awsworth Junction to Derby opened to all traffic in 1878. GNR activity in this part of Derbyshire no doubt influenced the Midland in its decision to reopen its Ilkeston branch to all traffic in 1880. The Midland, spurred on by having a rival in town, built a connecting line from the north to its station which it renamed Ilkeston Town. With a new line from Bennerley Junction to the Watnall Colliery branch, the Midland was able to offer an alternative route to Nottingham. However, the GNR route was quicker. Later renamed Ilkeston North, the station closed to passengers on 7 September 1964 and completely on 3 June 1968. (LGRP)

Heanor was the terminus of the GNR branch from Ilkeston via Nutbrook Colliery and Marpool. Opened for traffic in 1891, passenger services survived only a few decades, being withdrawn in the late 1930s. The station remained open for goods traffic until October 1963. (LGRP)

Railbuses stored out of use on the Friargate line were used for target practice by numerous children. (Chris Canner)

ACKNOWLEDGEMENTS

I would like to thank the following people for their help and encouragement: Tim Robinson, Baz Blood, Chris Elvidge and rest of my fellow former inmates at North West Freight (now EWS Railways). Thanks to Derek Gibson and Douglas Whitworth. Also thanks to Vic Hall for the industrial photos and memories of the 1960s, Chris Canner for the haircuts, Chris Law for the beer and Tony Griffin for sharing his experiences as a railway enthusiast in the 1970s. A special thanks to Lawrence Knighton and Chris and Mike Bentley for letting me raid their collections. Thanks are also due to the editor of the *Derby Evening Telegraph*, the National Railway Museum and the Imperial War Museum for permission to use photographs belonging to their organizations. Last but by no means least a special thanks to Sue Morgan for allowing a Luddite like myself near her computer.